Austerity in the UK: Did the Coalition Government Deliver on its "Fiscal Mandate"?

Alal Uddin
Fred Day

Austerity in the UK: Did the Coalition Government Deliver on its "Fiscal Mandate"?

By Alal Uddin

and Fred Day

March 2020

Praescientia Press

"For Science and for Art"

This paperback edition first published in 2020
by Praescientia Press
© Uddin and Day 2020
The moral right of the authors has been asserted.
All right reserved. Without limiting the rights under copyright reserved above, no part of this publication may be reproduced, stored or introduced into a retrieval system, or transmitted, in any form or by any means (electronic, mechanical, photocopying, recording, or otherwise) without the prior written permission of both the copyright owner and the above publisher of this book.

ISBN: 9781798816523

Contents:

Introduction		6

Scope, Methodology and Historical Context
1	Research Objectives	13
2	Plan and Research Methodology	15
3	*A New Economic Model* and the Emergency Budget	29
4	Early Forecasts	34

Review of Economic Theory
5	Can Severe Fiscal Contractions be Expansionary?	37
6	The Lost Keynesian Legacy	45
7	Saving and Investment; Investment and Saving	49

An Assessment of Economic Policy
8	2010-2012: Weak Growth and Revised Assumptions	63
9	2013-2014: A Belated Recovery	69
10	"Britain is Turning a Corner"	76

Evaluation of Austerity in the UK
11	Austerity Scrutinised	85

12	Austerity and Ideology	102
13	Austerity's Impact Upon Society	115
14	Concluding Remarks	121

Appendix I - The 2010 Mais Lecture — 124

Appendix II – Thomas Hodgskin's Early Business Cycle Theory — 162

Bibliography — 168

Index of Names — 196

Introduction

This book has two focal purposes; whilst it is initially a review of economic theory, it is also an assessment of economic policy derived from that theory. Specifically, the 2010-2015 Conservative and Liberal Democrat coalition government's austerity measures and their intellectual foundations. As such it aims to effectually address four questions:

a) How successful was this austerity, based on its own terms of reference?

b) To what extent was the coalition able to reduce the deficit?

c) Why was deficit reduction prioritised?

d) What economic and social outcomes have followed as a result?

Within contemporary (i.e. mainstream) standard economic theory, there are two contradictory views upon the effects of budget cuts or as they are euphemistically called by some economists, fiscal consolidations.

In one view, where consumption is assumed to be a function of current income, the effect of a fiscal adjustment is to reduce national income. The initial fall in aggregate demand resulting from cuts in Government expenditure is magnified (through a negative multiplier effect) into a subsequent decrease in national income. In this way Government spending is understood to contribute positively to the economy, GDP, and aggregate wages.

The alternative interpretation, where consumption is theorised as a function of permanent income, fiscal policy has no effect on aggregate demand. Known as the *Expansionary Fiscal Consolidation Hypothesis,* this concept states that cuts in Government budgets are expansionary in the sense that they stimulate economic growth. Although this would only be the case where the indirect effect of austerity on expectations is effectively sufficient to offset the otherwise contractionary effects of the initial reductions in national income.

This second view informed many preliminary justifications and several forecasts of the effects of austerity. It was here believed that the effect of budget cuts on real income were minor (that is, that fiscal multipliers were small). From 2012 onwards, following the emergence of economic growth below forecast in many countries that had adjusted their budgets in accordance with this view, several of the assumptions underpinning this second view were subjected to scrutiny. Research showed that as Central Banks' discount rates neared their lower zero bound rates, monetary policy was ineffectual and that the potential for successful fiscal stimulus (and unsuccessful fiscal consolidation) was higher than normal.

A preponderance of research has shown that, as Keynes had originally argued,[1] and as many re-emphasised in 2010, the time for austerity was not during a bust, but rather a boom. During a downturn, business and consumer confidence, as well as interest rates, are typically too low for expansionary monetary policy to be effective. Further, its effectiveness tended to be curtailed by the widespread deleveraging that tends to follow a financial sector-led recession.

---

[1] In August 1931 a Conservative led National Coalition Government was formed. The Conservative elements of this new coalition instigated Austerity measures in response to the economic crisis (following the Wall Street Crash of 1929). Keynes attacked the *National* Government's budget, in particular the wage cuts for school-teachers and the reductions in the road building and house building programmes. He warned that this austere budget would not only cause deflation but also result in unemployment worsening.

The initial implementation of fiscal consolidation and the coalition's decision to persist with it in the face of this evident below forecast growth, were not being adequately justified by the subsequent economic circumstances. The UK still had significant "fiscal space" and faced low borrowing costs; which meant that as such, there was little danger of a loss of market confidence in the UK's sovereign debt. However, Austerity has had the effect of further entrenching financialisation in the UK economy, which has continued to increase inequality as well as reducing both *real* wages and the wage share of GDP.

UK GDP had been forecast to return to its pre-crisis peak in mid-2014,[2] in spite of, rather than because of fiscal consolidation; this remained the slowest economic recovery for over a century. The subsequent symptoms of the 2007-08 financial crisis – high public sector borrowing and net debt – have been addressed rather than its fundamental causes within the financial sector.

---

[2] The BBC (25th July 2014) reported Osbourne's pleasure at what he called a "major milestone", when the initial ONS GDP figures aligned with those of the first quarter 2008.

The overall effect has been that financial crises remain no less likely than before, and remain just as much of a threat to public finances. The policy response of this government showed that it had either learned the wrong lessons from the financial crisis or that it had taken advantage of the situation in order to use the crisis as an opportunity to implement policies in its aftermath that would not otherwise have been possible, in the sense of being politically too unpalatable.

Part One:

Scope, Methodology and Historical Context

Austerity has a number of definitions that refer to a range of concepts. The definition most commonly used, in the media and in public discourse, is in reference to budget cuts: as the scaling back of government expenditure. International authorities as well as policy (and research) institutes commonly refer to a programme of such cuts as fiscal adjustments or fiscal consolidation.

The other popular conception of austerity is as a phenomenon in political economy. Expansionary fiscal consolidation is the concept that cuts in government expenditure may lead, causally, to economic growth. This view, as Mark Blyth (2013) explained, derived from a number of disparate liberal traditions (as explained in Sections 5 and 7 below).

1. Research Objectives

Three key objectives outline the aims and scope of this study.

Our initial objective: – was to attempt to ascertain the justifications put forward for the cutbacks in public sector expenditure and the economic theories supported such actions, given that the Neoclassical and Keynesian theories each start from contrasting assumptions and foundations.

As such we begin by asking three critical questions:

i. Had the coalition government been correct to argue that the Labour Party had been profligate while in office?

ii. How did the UK's national debt proliferate?

iii. What implications can be surmised regarding the effectiveness of austerity in meeting its policy objectives?

The second objective: – Our chief, and titular, aim is to illustrate an assessment of the performance of the coalition government on its own terms. These objectives were those specified by the Chancellor (George Osbourne) in his original emergency budget statement of 2010. Although our analysis deliberately eschews engaging in the empirical testing of a hypothesis, the implications of austerity measures in the short and medium term will be considered narratively.

As such we ask two further critical questions:

iv. Did the Chancellor deliver with regard to the economic targets set out in his 2010 emergency budget statement to ensure: a balanced structural budget and a falling national debt as a percentage of GDP, by the end of his first term in power?

v. Why did the coalition favour fiscal consolidation rather than expansionary fiscal policy, as a means of recovery?

Our final objective: – Is to begin a review of the social and economic consequences of the Austerity project. Hence, we pose two final questions:

vi. What have been the outcomes of the government's programme of fiscal consolidation?

vii. What effect has the government's fiscal mandate had on the main economic indicators?

2 Plan and Research Methodology

Our exposition consists of four parts within which there are several Sections. We aim at a broad, heterodox appraisal of the coalition's austerity measures and their intellectual foundations.

Part I contextualises the subject matter. As such, Sections 1 and 2 outline the fundamental structure and design of tour inquiry. Sections 3 and 4 then respectively place austerity in its historical context and document some of the initial forecasts.

Part II serves to review the relevant economic theory. Thereby, Sections 5, 6 and 7 explain and discuss the political economy underpinning the arguments for and against austerity. The expansionary austerity hypothesis is contrasted with the original Keynesian defence of state expenditure, so as to demonstrate how austerity may or may not have proved successful.

Part III discusses assessments of austerity in light of changing economic circumstances between 2010 and 2015.

Section 8 considers the reassessments of fundamental assumptions in the wake of flatlining growth between 2010 and 2012. Section 9 discusses the economic recovery from 2013 onwards and assesses the extent to which a new economic model had been implemented. Section 10 reviews the coalition's defence of austerity in the wake of this belated recovery and questions the validity of its foundational assumptions.

Part IV is concerned with the consequences that have resulted and are likely to result from the government's austerity measures. Sections 11 and 12 scrutinise the government's position that austerity was unavoidable and evaluates the extent to which austerity has been ideological. Section 13 considers the effects of austerity that cannot be captured by quantitative analysis and concludes with an overall evaluation of austerity in the UK.

Section 14 briefly concludes the work by drawing the whole to a tidied end. It also remarks on the coalition's legacy apparently derived from its austerity policies.

2.1 Appendixes

The text of the 2010 Mais lecture delivered by George Osbourne is reproduced as our first Appendix given the crucial role it played in to the overall history of this particular bout of austerity.

Our second Appendix is an exposition of Thomas Hodgskin's Business Cycle theories of the mid-19th century, which akin to later Austrian Economic ideas, saw Government over-encouragement at the root of unsustainable credit expansion.

2.2 A Review of Austerity, its Causes and its Consequences

The subject of this work has had enduring relevance to current events; austerity continues to be a defining economic and political issue of our time in that it created an environment that culminated in the 2016 Brexit vote. This much is reflected in the fact that the coalition government made deficit reduction its overall policy objective and that "the cost of living crisis" remained one of the Labour Party's central concerns leading up to the 2015 general election (Balls, 2014).

Given its subject matter, this study is necessarily and intentionally heterodox and critically pluralist in its nature. Firstly, the "tough decisions" that the government spoke of making were not arrived at free of value judgements, nor can they be assessed as such.

Secondly, contrary to proponents of the neoclassical synthesis, it is assumed throughout that there is no single theoretical framework within which austerity may be assessed. It will be shown that in the final analysis, austerity, like any other fundamentally social phenomenon, is value-laden to its very core. Therefore, in order to get to the heart of what austerity means and its likely consequences, a non-positivist (i.e. interpretivist) stance has necessarily been adopted, which reaches conclusions according to and within a pluralistic framework.

2.3 Economism and Scientism

This interpretivist stance will, crucially, draw influence from the methodology suggested by Karl Polanyi in his seminal *The Great Transformation* (1944). Polanyi, taking a holistic approach, conceived the economy as being, by default, embedded within wider society. Economic activity takes place not in its own separate vacuum but within society and consequently, economic phenomena cannot be fully understood without reference to the social sphere within which it is embedded (Bălan, 2012, p.1).

The "economistic fallacy", as Polanyi described it,[3] refers to the ingrained habit of individuals in industrialised society to attribute what is true of the nature of a particular economy to the nature of human society as a whole (Polanyi, 1977, p.5-6).[4]

Whilst it is correct and proper to study people outside an economic context, there can be very little validity in studying the economy outside the social context upon which it is contingent.

> ... given the methodological and ontological standpoint that it embraces, the neoclassical theory constitutes the paradigmatic case of the economistic fallacy, analyzing as it does both market and non-market economic activities indiscriminately

---

[3] See "Beyond the Economistic Fallacy: The Holistic Social Science of Karl Polanyi," in T. Skocpol, ed., *Vision and Method in Historical Sociology* (1984, pp. 47-84)

[4] Although this criticism has been around from well before Polanyi. For example, in 1867, Thomas Hodgskin had criticised Adam Smith for jumping from "principle to a particular mode in which labour is applied in modern society and especially in our community" (Hodgskin, 1867, p.2.) Also see Day (2019, p.148).

through a formal choice-theoretic framework built upon the postulate of rational individual calculative behavior. In effect, it proceeds from Gary Becker's (1976, p.8) premise: "[the] economic approach [is] applicable to all human behavior." (Adaman & Madra, 2002, p.1046)

Our work thereby draws on an analysis ranging beyond "purely economic" terms, considering ideological, political, social and historical factors where relevant.

2.4 The Inescapability of Value Judgements

The basis upon which austerity measures were proposed and continue to be justified are not value free, nor were their theoretical underpinnings.

In the first instance, the decision to cut government expenditure rather than to raise taxation is a clear expression of values. The consequence of budget cuts is that public services are reduced in their coverage or abolished altogether. The implication is that the public must rely on themselves or others for access to these services, which given their nature, tend to be important. Those that are well-off are likely to remain largely unaffected though those on insecure or low incomes will be made worse off. Fiscal consolidation necessarily results in distributional effects, likely to lead to substantive increases in inequality.

Secondly, though orthodox economic theory claims to be free of values, it cannot be, as all theory is continuously rooted in (a myriad of) social structures.

> economic models that purport to avoid values while at the same time privileging certain behavioural traits, such as self-interest, can never hope to be value-free. As has often been said, the rejection of a norm is itself a norm. Abandoning the terrain of values is a position that is value-laden to the core. (Tsakalotos, 2005, p.896)

Keynesian theory evolved as a response to the Great Depression, and New Keynesian theory as a response to some perceived inconsistencies within Keynesianism. A formalist framework that purports to be free of values is itself expressing a system of values – chief among them being that it is value free, or "positive". As John Gray explained:

In Positivist methodology, social science is no different from natural science. The model for both is mathematics. Nothing can be known unless it can be quantified[5] ... the idea that mathematics is the ideal form of human knowledge proved most powerful in economics ... Without realising it – for few of them know anything of the history of thought, least of all in their own subject – the majority of economists have inherited their way of thinking from the positivists. (Gray, 2009, p.270-271)

Milton Friedman's essay on *The Methodology Of Positive Economics* in his 1953 Book - *Essays In Positive Economics* set out the point that economic theories should not be about the real world and effectively need to be, or can benefit from being, unrealistic:

---

[5] Stephen Gould, in his *The Mismeasurement of Man* (1996) made the point that:
> To the statistician's dictum that whatever exists can be measured, the factorist has added the assumption that whatever can be "measured" must (page 341)

> Truly important and significant hypotheses will be found to have "assumptions" that are wildly inaccurate descriptive representations of reality, and, in general, the more significant the theory, the more unrealistic the assumptions (Friedman, 1953, p.8)

Theoretical frameworks do not simply describe phenomena, but also seek to shape the world in their image. If the coalition government were politically neutral, it should not prefer any specific combination of measures aimed at reducing government expenditure. However, the government has openly stated its political leanings, which are intimately tied into its economic policies. Both coalition members had emphasised the need for a shift away from what they perceived as the profligacy of the previous government. They then sought to express their liberal character,[6] most noticeably in the form of the *Big Society*.

The success of liberal policy is contingent upon the extent of liberal social values. As such, the extent to which the

---

[6] Their liberal philosophical, rather than any Liberal or Liberal Democrat party political character.

coalition was successful in asserting its own blend of liberalism depended in turn upon the extent to which British society was and perhaps still is willing to participate. Citing Karl Polanyi, Fikret Adaman & Yahya Madra (A&M) explain that:

> "[A] principle of behavior, in order to become effective, requires the presence of some institutional structure" (1977, p.42). According to this perception, for instance, calculative rationality, one particular behavioral pattern among many, should be conceptualized as an outcome of the active participation of the subject in markets rather than as the product of an immutable and transhistorical human essence (Polanyi 1977; see also Amariglio and Callari 1993). (Adaman & Madra, 2002. p.1051)

2.5 Incommensurability and Methodological Pluralism

The [economic] movement of the thirties was an attempt to bring analysis to bear on actual problems. Discussion of an actual problem cannot avoid the question of what should be done about it; questions

> of policy involve politics (laissez-faire is just as much a policy as any other). Politics involve ideology; there is no such thing as a "purely economic" problem that can be settled by purely economic logic; political interests and political prejudice are involved in every discussion of questions. The participants in controversy divide themselves in schools – conservative or radical and ideology is apt to seep into logic. In economics, arguments are largely devoted, as in theology, to supporting doctrines rather than testing hypotheses. (Robinson, 1977, p.1318)

Austerity cannot be understood as a purely economic phenomenon. A full appreciation of the justifications advanced for and against austerity requires an examination of political, ideological and historical factors among many others. As such its investigation needs to be understood as Political Economy rather than the more simplistic Economics.

When David Cameron spoke of hard decisions "beginning to pay off" (BBC News, 2013a), he was expressing a view based on assumptions fundamentally opposed to that of Seumas Milne (2013), who had maintained that "austerity has delivered depression and a lost decade". Cameron's pronouncement bore more in common with the fundamental assumptions of certain members of the Labour Party such as Liz Kendall, when they argue that "any party that is serious about being in government will need to take difficult decisions" (Watt, 2012).

The vanity of applying a single, formalist methodology is perhaps best explained by the conflict between the central assumptions of the two main schools of economic thought considered here. The case for expansionary fiscal consolidation is essentially unintelligible within a Keynesian framework, where a decrease in aggregate expenditure (or an increase in saving) leads necessarily to a lower national income. However, understood through neoclassical theory, where the Law of Markets is implicitly assumed, fiscal consolidation could theoretically lead to an expansion.

Therefore, it is assumed throughout – in opposition to the New Keynesian view – that neoclassical and Keynesian frameworks are all fundamentally incommensurable and as such, must be considered on their own terms rather than through the adoption of a "one size fits all" approach. In more explicit terms, this investigation will not be approached in the positive manner argued for by Milton Friedman. For instance, it is assumed that here in political economy, the broader context is crucial and that descriptively false assumptions (for instance, rational expectations) categorically cannot yield meaningful conclusions – further still, that this approach is scientistic.

> As Marx says somewhere, microscopes and chemical reagents are not appropriate to the analysis of economic forms. I suspect most of us would agree with this assessment. But the point is a general one. All methods of analysis are appropriate to some sorts of material but not others. This is as true of mathematical methods as others. My claim here is that the explanation of the poor showing of much of modern economics is that mathematical methods are being imposed in situations for which they are largely inappropriate. (Lawson, 2006)

All our discussions henceforth set out to be methodologically pluralistic. The overarching concern is to evaluate policies, concepts, arguments and schools of thought on their own terms as far as possible; and where not possible, to arrive at judgements based on sound reasoning.

2.6 A Holistic Framework

Given the inescapability of values, we necessarily eschew a positivist methodology in favour of an interpretivist framework. The research aims are met not through the indiscriminate application of scientific methods but rather a holistic framework that emphasises and appreciates the complexity of the issues concerned. As Bălan explains:

> every part of a system can be understood only by reference to the whole, because its existence and proper functioning depend on the fact that it is not an isolated entity, but a part of the system. (Bălan, 2012, p.1)

This framework draws influence predominantly from the thought and ideas of Karl Polanyi, who, In contrast to neoclassical economists' attempts to implant society within the economy, emphasised the embeddedness of the economic system within the wider social sphere.

Austerity cannot be fully understood without reference to its fundamental causes and policy aims. The events that led to the build-up of the national debt are crucial to understanding the motives for austerity and its likely consequences.

3. *A New Economic Model* and the Emergency Budget

In September 2007, in the wake of the crisis in North American sub-prime mortgage lending, Northern Rock had applied to the Bank of England for emergency liquidity; news reports of this sparked fears of its bankruptcy and ultimately, the first run on a British bank for over a century. In February 2008, Northern Rock was eventually nationalised, followed by Bradford & Bingley in September and the bailouts of Royal Bank of Scotland, Lloyds TSB and HBOS in October (BBC, 2008; Kingsley, 2012).

This was a financial crisis with deep and lasting repercussions. The financial costs of the bailouts, partial and full nationalisations and deficit expenditure aimed at shoring up economic confidence were immense. The National Audit Office (NAO, 2010, p.6) evaluated the maximum cost to the UK taxpayer as £512 billion, approximately a fifth of UK GDP in 2014.

In political terms, the incumbent government, not surprisingly, suffered a severe loss in its credibility, which continues to haunt politics to the present day.

While emphasising the global nature of the crisis, the then Prime Minister, Gordon Brown, accepted responsibility for the loose regulation that allowed banks to take excessive risks in lending and investment – much of which Lord Turner described as "socially useless" (Inman, 2009). The acceptance of the failings of loose regulation was perhaps more politically palatable than actually acknowledging the fundamental systemic failings and faults that are endemic within modern financial systems.

Not long after the financial system had (apparently) been adequately rehabilitated, there was a swift turn in mood – away from deficit expenditure and towards an emphasis on financial and fiscal reform in the lead-up to the 2010 general election. Brown maintained that budget cuts would be damaging economically, and that growth must be prioritised in order to reduce the deficit in a socially just manner.

> "There are some who say we must plan for a decade of austerity. If that

happened, it would also be a decade of unfairness, where while the privileged few can protect themselves but the majority lose out." (BBC News, 2009)

Brown's Labour Chancellor Alistair Darling however, acknowledged the opposition view that cuts were "never negotiable" and that "once recovery is established, we have to act", aiming to halve the deficit over four years (BBC News, 2010a).

In his 2010 Mais Lecture speech [24th February 2010 – see Appendix III], the then Shadow Chancellor George Osborne had argued that the economy must head in a new direction.

> Britain has been failed by the economic policy framework of the last decade. It promised stability, prudence and an end to the cycle - it delivered instability, imprudence and the biggest boom followed by the deepest bust. We need to head in a completely new direction … We have to move away from an economic model that was based on unsustainable private and public debt … This will require new policies and new institutions.

> First, a new approach to macroeconomic and financial policy, where we seek to contain credit cycles as well as target price stability. Second, a new fiscal policy framework, with an independent Office for Budget Responsibility to ensure that public debt is sustainable. And third, a supply side revolution that releases the pent-up enterprise and wealth creation of our country (Osborne, 2010a)

A Conservative government would, he argued, be more fiscally responsible, rebalance the economy away from debt-fuelled expenditure and oversee a supply side recovery.[7] Further, he argued that these reforms were not simply desirable but necessary, in order to strengthen market confidence in the country's public finances amid fears that the European sovereign debt crisis might spread to the UK.

In May 2010, following a hung parliament, the Conservatives and the Liberal Democrats formed a coalition

---

[7] Despite these ambitions, subsequent experience however has seen increased private indebtedness.

government. In their emergency budget statement to the House of Commons, Chancellor George Osborne announced sweeping reforms, which he argued would deal:

> decisively with our country's record debts ... at the very moment when fear about the sustainability of sovereign debt is the greatest risk to the recovery of European economies (Osborne 2010b).

The coalition government's fiscal mandate – the government's primary objective for the public finances – would be forward–looking (rather than backward) and assessed not by the Chancellor, but the autonomous *Office for Budget Responsibility* (OBR), in contrast with Gordon Brown's *Golden Rule*. Its formal mandate was announced as follows:

> the structural current deficit should be in balance in the final year of the five-year forecast period, which is 2015-16 in this Budget. (Ibid.)

Osborne stated that the government's prioritisation of deficit reduction was determined in response to the international consensus formed at the 2010 Toronto summit of the G20,[8] where it was agreed that countries with budget surpluses should work towards increasing their expenditure and that deficit countries should appropriately adjust their budgets. In the light of this new consensus, and to emphasis the coalition's commitment to fiscal responsibility, a further economic objective was announced:

> In order to place our fiscal credibility beyond doubt, this mandate will be supplemented by a fixed target for debt, which in this Parliament is to ensure that debt is falling as a share of GDP by 2015-16. (Ibid.)

4. Early Forecasts

The OBR's initial assessment was bullish, predicting the coalition's achievement of a balanced structural current budget and a falling national debt level by 2014-15, one year earlier than originally targeted.

In its 2010 Budget Forecast, the OBR (2010, p.80-82) predicted economic growth of 1.2 per cent in 2010, 2.3 per cent in 2011 and the adjustment of growth to its trend rate from 2013 onwards. Inflation, as measured by the Consumer Prices Index

---

[8] Held on 26th to 27th June 2010.

(CPI), was expected to fall from around 3 per cent in 2011 to a "little under 2 per cent in early 2012" before settling at its target rate (2%) in the medium term. Employment was expected to rise rapidly from 2011 onwards in conjunction with the upturn in growth, reaching 30 million by 2015.[9]

> Wages and salaries growth rises gradually throughout the forecast, reaching 5½ percent in 2014. Consumption growth rises in the forecast to rates of over 2 per cent from 2013, but it remains below the rate of growth of GDP. (2010, p.83)

Business investment was expected to improve steadily, rising 1.5 per cent in 2010 and between 8-11 per cent from 2011 onwards, boosted by the reduction in corporation tax.

> Business investment also strengthens as resources released from the government sector flow into the private sector. (Ibid.)

---

[9] ONS figures for October 2015 state a figure 31,122,000 in employment at that point. This had risen further to 32,597,000, to much Conservative government fanfare, by February 2019.

Forecasts of economic growth and the depreciation of sterling were expected to feed through to an improvement in net exports with a narrowing of the trade deficit over the forecast period and a near-balancing of the current account by 2015. (Ibid, p.84)

In their initial assessments, two of the three main credit rating agencies, Moody's and Fitch, praised the coalition government's austerity drive, agreeing that austerity measures would meet their aims.

> "The UK economy appears sufficiently flexible and robust to grow moderately, even in the face of … austere fiscal consolidation" … The British government has enjoyed a AAA rating from Moody's ever since it first received a long-term debt rating in 1978 (BBC News, 2010b)

> "[The] budget statement is a strong statement of intent by the new UK government to accelerate the path of deficit reduction and stabilise and reduce the public debt burden," Fitch credit rating agency said. (Moya, 2010)

Part Two:
Review of Economic Theory

This part of our research is concerned with our first research objective. The economic theory underpinning the arguments for and against austerity will be introduced, explained and contrasted here. Together, these sections demonstrate how and why the coalition may or may not have delivered on its fiscal mandate.

5. Can Severe Fiscal Contractions be Expansionary?

The drive for austerity in the UK derived its intellectual authority above all from a body of literature on expansionary fiscal consolidation – at the forefront of which was the work of Alberto Alesina (Elliott, 2013a), who in turn, built on research carried out by Francesco Giavazzi and Marco Pagano (G&P) (1990). This section starts by investigating the assumption that fiscal consolidation is necessary and how it might successfully lead to an economic recovery.

5.1 There Was No Alternative

> an anticyclical fiscal policy based upon spending increases in recessions and tax increases to correct the deficits during expansions is likely to be counterproductive in addition to implying a creeping up of the size of government already around 50 per cent of GDP or more in European countries. (Alesina, 2010: 15)

In a speech delivered to the April 2010 meeting of the Directorate General for Economic and Financial Affairs (ECFIN) of the European Commission, Alesina argued that fiscal consolidation was imperative for the euro area member states. The experiences of inter-war hyperinflation and the post-war golden age of economic growth "do not offer much guidance for today". The high national debt levels experienced by European countries necessitated budget cuts, he argued; further, evidence suggested that cuts may not necessarily result in recession.

5.2 The Expansionary Austerity Hypothesis

Giavazzi and Pagano (1990) examined this aforementioned hypothesis, pointing to two episodes in Denmark and Ireland in the 1980s that they argued contradicted the Keynesian orthodoxy, which stated that cuts were contractionary. They contrasted two positions from the outset – the "Keynesian view" and that of the German Council of Economic Experts (an anti-Keynesian view) – and argued that while the "German view" may run counter to conventional (i.e. Keynesian) wisdom, there was evidence that it was valid.

> The German Council of Economic Experts [Sachverstandigenrat] ... proposed [in 1981] the view that the impact of budget deficits on demand was predominantly negative, so that fiscal retrenchment should be seen as the premise for an expansion, rather than a recession. (Giavazzi and Pagano, 1990, p.75)

Giavazzi and Pagano cited Hellwig and Neumann (1987, p.187-88) in explaining how such fiscal consolidations may have indirect expansionary effects on output through the expectations (or confidence) channel:

> The direct demand impact of slower public expenditure growth is clearly negative ... The indirect effect on aggregate demand of the initial reduction in expenditure growth

> occurs through an improvement in expectations if the measures taken are understood to be part of a credible medium-run program of consolidation, designed to permanently reduce the share of government in GDP ... [and thus] taxation in the future. (Giavazzi and Pagano, 1990, p.76)

That is, there can be a positive indirect effect on aggregate demand if the public believes the programme of fiscal consolidation to be credible, i.e. that it will result in a permanent reduction in taxation (a permanent reduction in the size of the public sector) and thereby an increase in their permanent income. This effect on expectations was enough, Giavazzi and Pagano argued, to offset the initial contractionary effect on aggregate demand, in such a way as to lead to an economic expansion. Further, they reasoned that the experiences of both Denmark and Ireland in the 1980s provided evidence for this view.

They also argued that the 1984-86 consumption boom in Denmark could not be explained fully by the wealth effects which followed a fall in interest rates. There was a component of this boom, they contended, which could only be explained by the German view: that budget cuts signalled an increase in individuals' permanent income which increased current consumption.

Giavazzi and Pagano found no such evidence of an expectations effect in the first stabilisation in Ireland, which they claimed is explained by constraints on liquidity at the time. Irish consumers may have expected to pay less in future taxation, though they were unable to increase their current consumption due to incomplete access to credit – something that they believed may have been resolved by the time the second Irish fiscal adjustment took effect. Further, they argued, the consumption boom following the second Irish adjustment might be explained by that subsequent adjustment consisting of a greater reduction in spending than the first.

Ultimately, Giavazzi and Pagano believed that the fiscal consolidations in Denmark and Ireland were expansionary and that the most important factor involved was the credibility of the adjustments, as this formed the basis for rational consumers to expect lower future taxation, thereby increasing current consumption. This would be via the medium of credit, effectively secured against the expectation that impeding tax cuts would effectively increase future incomes.

The IMF's Chief Economist (2008-2015) Olivier Blanchard had previously commended (1990) the work of Giavazzi and Pagano for demonstrating ways in which non-Keynesian effects may result from expenditure cuts – he found that the cases of Denmark and Ireland in the 1980s showed that the German view is "sometimes" right.

Alberto Alesina and Silvia Ardagna (A&A) (2009) built upon the work by Giavazzi and Pagano, arguing that fiscal adjustments are most effective where they involve large changes in government expenditure that are implemented early on, as this increased the credibility of such adjustments. That is, Alesina and Ardagna supported front-loaded fiscal consolidation, as this spells out to the general public (i.e. consumers) that the government was serious about reducing the national debt and had committed itself wholeheartedly to a programme that would achieve its objectives and thus be able to lower the tax burden. They found in their research that adjustments based on spending cuts alone are more likely to reduce deficits and national debt than those based on tax increases and that tax cuts are more likely to increase growth more than spending increases. Further, expenditure cuts might be not only the way forward to a more 'normal' state of public finances, but also an expansion in economic growth.

The mechanism through which expansions may be generated was, again, the expectations channel. This analysis is built on Friedmanite assumptions: rational individuals, once they have become aware of credible and substantial cuts in government expenditure, understand that their permanent income will increase and consequently, increase their current consumption, either by decreased savings or increased borrowing.

5.3 **Neoliberalism**

The neoliberal or "New Treasury" view as it was described by King et al (2012) shared many basic similarities with more traditional strands of economic liberalism and the original Treasury View. The current episode, could arguably, be seen as increasingly resembling the inter-war period.

In that era, rational self-interest was seen as the driving force of economic activity. It was believed that the private sector, if left to its own devices would lead to allocative efficiency – that supply created its own demand and as such, there could not be a deficiency of demand.

This is the modern interpretation of Say's Law. It is not so much a statement that whatever is supplied will be sold. Rather that whatever is supplied could be sold if the price is sufficiently lowered so as to equilibrate with prospective purchasers' valuations. It is based on a notion of Instrumental Rationality whereby a rational person would accept what the market (an Efficient Market) would deem as the *correct* Price.

Thus, when Labour is unemployed, it must be because the Labourers are unprepared to work for the market derived *correct* price. As accepting the market price is a freely entered into choice in market economies, there can never be any Involuntary Unemployment. Everybody can find work if they are only willing to work for low enough wages. Hence, perhaps, the emergence of the co-called Gig Economy is this theory being again put into practice.

In this view, economic growth is necessarily supply-led; demand management can only lead to growth through budget cuts. Further, the state should balance its budget in order that it does not crowd out private investment.

In the current period, rational self-interest is in fact understood not only as the driving force of economic activity, but all activity. James Buchanan once argued that there was no collective public interest; Thatcher is renowned for arguing that there was no such thing as society. These are no longer fringe beliefs.[10] The coalition government based its economic strategy on this view, pledging a "new economic model" involving a supply-led recovery.

Lord Freud, the welfare reform minister, exemplified this view when he asserted in the House of Lords that welfare was no longer, if indeed it ever was, fundamentally social in its nature but rather motivated equally by rational self-interest.

6. The Lost Keynesian Legacy

This section considers the contrary view, as identified, for example, by Robert

---

[10] As Polanyi predicted society has become embedded in the economy, rather than the economy being embedded in society. i.e. society has become subservient to the market, rather than the market being subservient to society's needs. This indeed is the major eponymous element of his *Great Transformation* (1944).

Boyer (2012). He identified and explained four fallacies that he argued would, in the general case, result in the failure rather than success of austerity measures. The instances of successful expansionary austerity, Boyer maintained, were special cases that cannot be generalised across the global economy.

To the extent that it may be successful, austerity was dependent upon three possible mechanisms:

The first concerned a rivalry between public and private financing; a case where state borrowing can be shown to have a crowding out effect.

The second was the case where forward-looking individuals, with full access to credit, increased their consumption as a response to the reduction in public spending (the converse of the Ricardian equivalence theorem).

The third was the possibility of an export-led recovery, which might offset any contraction in domestic consumption. However, Boyer cautioned that:

> there is no general theoretical reason to guarantee the success of any austerity policy. Everything depends on how all these opposite

effects interact. In some configurations, they may even succeed in restoring public finance credibility, whereas in others they may fail. (Boyer, 2012, p.297)

6.1 **The Four Fallacies of Contemporary Austerity Measures**

Boyer argued that the case for austerity rested upon some fundamental misunderstandings of the macroeconomy that were addressed by Keynes in the *The General Theory* (*TGT*), which have been largely forgotten and misrepresented in such a way as to give credence to damaging pre-Keynesian notions.

The first fallacy was that austerity measures presume a budgetary populism that in most countries did not exist. Fiscal consolidation as such, is an improper response to high national debt in countries like the UK, where the build-up of debt has been a consequence of banking failures rather than public sector profligacy.

The second fallacy was the notion of expansionary fiscal consolidation, from which it follows that budget cuts may be expansionary when implemented by many countries simultaneously. This notion "neglects the short-term negative effects on domestic demand and overestimates the generality of Ricardian equivalence" (Boyer, 2012, p.283).

The third fallacy was the insistence on a universal application of austerity measures regardless of the initial causes of high national debt and as such, represented a repetition of the error of the Washington consensus, "namely the 'one size fits all approach" (Ibid, p.310).

> Greece and Portugal cannot replicate the hard-won German success. Their productive, institutional and political configurations differ drastically and, thus, they require different policies. (Ibid, p.283)

Finally, austerity measures, far from being unavoidable or benign, risked tipping Europe back into the dangerous "beggar-thy-neighbour" of the inter-war period.

> The idea that if all economies repeat the strategy that has proven to be efficient for an individual country the world economy will recover is actually a fourth fallacy. This notion is an extension at the international level of the fallacy of composition

that is at the core of Keynesian macroeconomics. (Ibid., p.306)

Boyer concluded that the power of the international finance community had led to its capture of macroeconomic theorising and that the consequent return of pre-Keynesian theory may well become a contributing factor to the next major financial crisis (Ibid, p.311).

7. Saving and Investment

At the heart of the arguments for and against austerity were the contrasting assumptions of two economists: Jean-Baptiste Say and John Maynard Keynes. Arguments in favour of budget cuts are explicable with reference to the Law of Markets; arguments cautioning against fiscal retrenchment are best understood with reference to the fallacy of composition at the heart of *The General Theory*.

Within the neoclassical paradigm – where markets inevitably clear and there is an inescapable tendency towards equilibrium at full employment – an increase in saving leads instantaneously to an increase in investment through a change in the rate of interest (a clearing of the market for loanable funds). In the Keynesian paradigm, the notion that a lower interest rate would re-equilibrate saving and investment is disputed; cheaper loanable funds are not incentive enough to invest. The rationale is as follows:

> Why sink a lot of money into plant and equipment when your factory and machines are half idle? Even when interest rates are low, firms won't invest unless it is profitable for them to do so. (Slavin, 2009, p.261)

In this paradigm, where national income is determined through expenditure, it is investment that generates saving (Robinson, 1972, p.9), through the multiplier effect. An increase in investment leads to a magnified increase in national income; the majority of the increase is consumed but part of it is saved. An increase in saving has the opposite effect, leading to a lower national income and lower investment.

The importance of these contrasting views lies in their implied conclusions with respect to the role of the state. In the Keynesian view, where irreducible uncertainty leads necessarily to fundamental market instability, the state has an essential role in maintaining stability. In the neoclassical view, where the market economy is fundamentally self-correcting, only a basic state is necessary in order to protect property rights and correct certain market failures.

In other words, in the neoclassical view, government cuts are not problematic as the private sector is without doubt sufficiently dynamic to generate supply-led growth and regulate itself. Fiscal consolidation may even be beneficial as some of the more "unproductive" aspects of government expenditures will be purged. In the Keynesian view, the timing of cuts is crucial as a reduction in any one of the four components of aggregate demand will result in a magnified decrease in national income. If public spending is cut during a boom, business and consumer confidence should remain largely unaffected. In a downturn, budget cuts could lead to a full-blown depression.

7.1 The Demise of the Loanable Funds Concept

Interestingly the BoE has, for example in its Quarterly Bulletin for the first quarter of 2014, acknowledged the Post-Keynesian position that "Saving does not by itself increase the deposits or 'funds available' for banks to lend" (McLeay et al, 2014, p.15). The BoE Staff Working Paper No. 529 – *Banks are not intermediaries of loanable funds - and why this matters* – again emphasised this point:

> The currently dominant intermediation of loanable funds (ILF) model views banks as barter institutions that intermediate deposits of pre-existing real loanable funds between depositors and borrowers. The problem with this view is that, in the real world, there are no pre-existing loanable funds, (Jakab and Kumhof, 29th May 2015, p.38)

This position was backed up in their BoE Staff Working Paper No. 761: *Banks are not intermediaries of loanable funds — facts, theory and evidence* (January, 2019). Here it was concluded that loanable funds concept "as a modelling shortcut this is unrealistic and has unrealistic implications." (Jakab and Kumhof, January 2019, p.30)

7.2 Austerity and Say's Law

Steven Kates (2012) hailed Alesina's work for its ground-breaking theoretical and policy implications. He took the view that government deficit expenditure cannot increase employment through a multiplier effect and argued for a revival in the classical theory which enabled a proper understanding of Alesina's work.

> If one understood the classical law of markets, what is today called Say's Law, there one would find an explanation for why cuts to public spending and a lowering of the deficit would lead to an increase in economic activity and a rise in employment. There would be found why an expansion of unproductive spending would lead to a worsening of economic conditions and a rise in unemployment. If one understands that demand comes only from increases in value adding supply, then one begins to understand why non-productive forms of stimulus spending would not only fail to achieve the results they were intended to achieve but would, in fact, make economic conditions worse than they already were. (Kates, 2012, p.413)

Kates explained that it was only through a more productive composition of GDP (a shift towards a greater private sector share of output) that a sustainable recovery was possible. This was the reasoning behind Alesina's insistence that welfare budgets cannot be left untouched (Alesina, 2010, p.10) and the coalition's emphasis on an enterprise-led recovery.

However, this view seems not to take into consideration the modern developments of Financialisation, whereby productive firms are increasingly superseded by financial institutions or firms more concerned with financial matters than traditional productivity.

7.3 **The Classical Debate on what is Productive**

Kates' appeal to a revival of Classical Economics's distinction of Productive and Unproductive, in terms of Government spending is grounded in that paradigm's earlier views (Smith and Say) rather than Classical Economics' mature perspective where such a distinction was effectively dismissed as flawed. Only initially were Classical Economists concerned with the issues and implications of productive and unproductive labour.

For example, Piercy Ravenstone, who in his *Thoughts on the Funding System* (1824), still adhered to the concept of productive and unproductive labour, and saw that productive labour decreased and that unproductive labour increased as a result of capital accumulation.

However for Hodgskin the branding of employment as productive or non-productive was a false distinction that further helped capitalists to justify exaggerated profits. For Hodgskin all labour expended was characterized as productive if the labourer made a living as a result.

> No industry is unproductive but that, the product of which no person will buy, and which does not contribute to the individual's subsistence or gratification. (Hodgskin, 1827, p.50)

Returning to his axiom that "we live by the sweat of our brow" the labour that enabled life to persist must be productive, if it were capable of supporting and re-producing that life.

> The object in labouring is to supply the individual's wants. Nature gave him his faculties and powers for this purpose; for this purpose only, and not for the purpose of supplying the wants of other men whom she equally endowed. If his labour, in addition to supplying his own wants, will supply the wants of other persons, will enable him to rear up a family, and pay taxes, rent, and profit, so much the better: the

society may increase the faster; but if his labour is not so productive, if it only enable him to subsist, replacing whatever tools, seed, corm &c., so that his condition is not gradually deteriorated, his labour is productive. (Hodgskin, 1827, p.50-1)

Hodgskin was not alone in this as illustrated by Scrope's 1831 article, *The Political Economists*, in the *Quarterly Review,* that seemed to concur with Hodgskin that all labour was productive:–

We think there can be no difficulty in defining productive labour to be that of which the result is a *saleable* article: it will include that of professional persons, officers of government, authors, artists, merchants, tradesmen, labourers, &c. Unproductive occupations (for, correctly speaking, all *labour* is productive) are those which are productive only of gratification to the agent (Scrope, 1831, p.6).

Nassau Senior (1836) concluded that although the separation of productive and unproductive labour was due to the arbitrariness of language and social relations.

In J.S. Mill's essay *On the Words Productive and Unproductive* (1844) Mill had highlighted the crucial issue with Classical Economist's use of these terms:

> It would probably be difficult to point out any two words, respecting the proper use of which political economists have been more divided, than they have been concerning the two words *productive* and *unproductive*; whether considered as applied to *labour*, to *consumption*, or to *expenditure*. (Mill, vol. IV, p.281)

Mill' definitive Classical Economic discussion of productive and unproductive makes clear the developed Classical Economist's position:

> This use of the terms, therefore, is subversive of the ends of language. ... Every classification according to which a basket of cherries, gathered and eaten the next minute, are called wealth, while that title is denied to the acquired skill of those who are acknowledged to be productive labourers, is a purely arbitrary division, and does not conduce to the ends for which

classification and nomenclature are designed.

Presumably Mill was referring to absurdity of the early Classical Economists' classification of medical doctors, teachers, lawyers and presumably Economists, as unproductive. It may be to this that Kates was referring to. However, this might explain the subsequent austerity measures applied to the first three of these particular areas of Government expenditure.

7.4 The Contemporary Intellectual History of Austerity

As Mark Blyth (2013a) explained, the expansionary austerity hypothesis was rooted among a series of disparate strands of liberalism which each contributed to the notion of a large state sector as problematic.

In the ordoliberal tradition, the state does not lead economic development, but supports it by enforcing a constitution, which: enforces competition, maintains price stability (through an independent central bank with low and stable inflation as its sole mandate) and generates economic growth through the production of competitive, high quality goods and services:

> whereby the quality of the products manufactured would create the demand for them, in a modern supply side restatement of Say's law. (Blyth, 2013a, p.137)

The Austrian school, founded by Karl Menger in the late nineteenth century, had a similarly restrained role for the state. This school of thought, Blyth explained, saw the economy as having a long-run evolutionary structure that state intervention could only harm (Ibid., p.144).

Its theory of the business cycle explained the bust as the end result of an expansion in credit that distorts the signalling effect of the rate of interest, in turn misleading entrepreneurs as to the underlying social rate of time preference, leading to malinvestments.[11] In this view, austerity is just what the economy needs in a downturn, in order for prices to adjust to their true values. If banks are in danger of going bust, they should be allowed to fail

---

[11] See Appendix I – *Thomas Hodgskin's Early Business Cycle Theory – based on Government encouraged Credit Expansion* for a discussion of Thomas Hodgskin's Austrian-like business cycle ideas.

as intervention would only exacerbate the business cycle. The economy, at its core, can and must be allowed to correct itself.

What enabled the German and Austrian justifications for austerity to take on a popular global appeal, explained Blyth, were the broader ideological and institutional shifts of the 1970s: the rise to prominence of neoliberalism, a view amounting to:

> a complex fusion of monetarism (Friedman), rational expectations (Robert Lucas), public choice (James Buchanan, and Gordon Tullock), and the less respectable but by no means uninfluential 'supply-side' ideas of Arthur Laffer ... The more acceptable commonality to these arguments was that government intervention was the problem rather than the solution, and that 'a stable monetary policy, plus radical tax cuts in the top brackets, would produce a healthier economy' by getting the incentives for entrepreneurial activity aligned correctly (Harvey, 2005, p.54)

What united these ideas and made them politically powerful was their

> joint production of the state as the inflationary pump rather than the economic shock absorber. By painting the state in this way, they made the state "doing more" a dangerous idea (Blyth, 2013, p.152)

The fall of the Berlin Wall in 1989 and the disintegration of the former Soviet Union in the early 1990s marked the beginning of another important stage towards contemporary austerity policies. The Washington Consensus, as it became known, was intended as a list of ten policies that embodied the shift away from the old ideas of development economics, capturing "the essential features of what we now call austerity policies rather well" (Ibid.: 161). These policies, which had been designed as a response to the Latin American debt crisis became in Blyth's words, "the instruction sheet applied to any developing or transitioning economy in the 1990s".

The turn to austerity then, Blyth argued, following what appeared to be an initial return to Keynesian demand management in the wake of the 2007-08 financial crisis, came almost as a natural response, given the dominance of neoliberalism in the preceding decades. Policymakers gripped by these ideas could not envision any response other than the restoration of pre-crisis public finances through fiscal consolidation (Chowdhury & Islam, 2012).

Part Three:

An Assessment of Economic Policy

This part of our work is concerned with our second objective - our principal aim to achieve an assessment of the performance of the coalition government on its own terms. The following sections discuss the latter shift in consensus about the effects of fiscal consolidation on economic growth and consider the extent to which the success of austerity is dependent upon the business cycle.

8. 2010-2012: Weak Growth and Revised Assumptions

While many early forecasts were optimistic, ultimately, economic growth in the UK was below forecast over the period 2010-12, with annual rates of 1.7 per cent in 2010, 1.1 per cent in 2011 and 0.3 per cent in 2012 (World Bank); per capita growth figures were equally disappointing.

Consequently, the OBR was forced to concede in its December 2012 Economic and Fiscal Outlook (EFO) that two years into its first term, the coalition government would not be able to meet its primary objective of balancing the structural budget, either by 2014-15 (as it had forecast in 2010) or 2015-16 (the end of the five-year forecast period). As a result, neither would the coalition be able to deliver a falling national debt level by 2015-16.

> The Government's 'fiscal mandate' requires it to balance the cyclically-adjusted current budget (CACB) at the end of a rolling five-year period, now 2017-18. Our central forecast shows the CACB in surplus by 0.9 per cent of GDP in 2017-18, implying that the Government is more likely than not to meet the mandate.
>
> The Government now appears more likely than not to miss its 'supplementary target', which requires PSND [Public Sector Net Debt] to fall as a share of GDP between 2014-15 and 2015-16. (OBR, 2012, p.6)

This weakness in economic growth was also a key factor in both Moody's and Fitch downgrading the UK credit rating, from AAA to AA1 and AA+ respectively.

> Moody's Investor Services downgraded the UK from AAA to AA1 ... citing "continuing weakness in the UK's medium-term growth outlook" and concerns over debt levels. (Armitstead, 2013)

This was a distinct failure with regards to the Chancellor's aspirations set out in his Mais lecture where he claim his policies would "maintain Britain's AAA credit rating" (Osbourne, 2010b).

8.1 Growth Forecast Errors and Fiscal Multipliers

Flatlining economic growth in the OECD world led Olivier Blanchard and Daniel Leigh (B&L) (2013) and Oscar Jorda and Alan Taylor (J&T) (2013) to conclude that the negative effects of fiscal consolidation on growth had been underestimated.

Blanchard and Leigh found that generally, in countries which had planned fiscal consolidations, economic growth had been lower than forecast. The natural interpretation, they argued, was that fiscal multipliers are higher than they were assumed to be. Three reasons were put forward in explanation:

Firstly, at the zero lower bound (of interest rates), monetary policy is all but ineffective in boosting aggregate demand.

Secondly, lower GDP, coupled with a failing financial system, led to consumption and investment being more dependent upon savings and retained profits rather than future income.

Finally, recent research had shown that fiscal multipliers are larger in periods where significant spare capacity exists.

Blanchard and Leigh concluded that fiscal multipliers were indeed higher than previously thought: "actual multipliers ... were substantially above 1 in the early years of the crisis" (Blanchard and Leigh, 2013, p.6).

Assessing the impact of austerity in the UK, Jorda and Taylor modelled the path of GDP growth both in the existence and absence of the coalition government's economic measures. Their Figure 4, from their paper (2013, p.27) showed their results: real GDP had been far lower than forecast by the OBR, with 3 percentage points of lost GDP accounted for by the effects of austerity measures.

They displayed the unconditional forecast path in a financial crisis recession based on the large sample of all advanced-economy recessions since 1870 in the work of Jorda, Schularick, and Taylor (2011), extended to the six-year horizon. Much of the dismal performance can thereby be attributed to the fiscal policy choice of instigating austerity during the slump.

8.2 The Timing of Austerity

Nitika Bagaria et al (2012) considered the effects on GDP of the coalition's planned fiscal consolidation in three scenarios: as it occurred; delayed by three years; in its absence. They concluded that in the absence of fiscal consolidation, national debt as a percentage of GDP increased. In other words, the question was not if government spending should be cut but rather when. They also found that a consolidation in "normal times" was less detrimental to GDP than the same consolidation during a depression. In their evaluation, while in the long run there were no significant hysteresis effects:

> the economic pain resulting from fiscal consolidation could not have been avoided, but could have been substantially reduced. The standard policy prescription – to delay deficit reduction until after recovery is

clearly under way and the output shortfall significantly reduced – remains valid (Bagaria et al, 2012).

The coalition had always maintained, publicly and officially, that austerity had not been detrimental to economic growth, however, the Prime Minister found himself challenged on this matter in 2013 by Robert Chote, the Chairman of the OBR. While Cameron had stated publicly that in its independent judgement, growth had been slower than forecast as a result of difficulties in the euro area, rising oil prices and the overhang from the financial crisis, Chote made clear that:

> ... every forecast published by the OBR since the June 2010 Budget has incorporated the widely held assumption that tax increases and spending cuts reduce economic growth in the short term. (Chote, 2013)

Most notably of all, the IMF had disputed the coalition's view; its Managing Director Christine Lagarde argued that in light of the research conducted by Blanchard and Leigh, the pace of fiscal consolidation in the UK should have been eased:

"We have said that should growth abate, should growth be particularly low, then there should be consideration to adjusting by way of slowing the pace. This is nothing new. And this is still the position and one that has been very clearly articulated within the various departments. So we very much stand by that." (Elliott, 2013b)

The IMF's Chief Economist Olivier Blanchard was clearer still, commenting that if the UK continued with its fiscal consolidation as planned, it was "playing with fire" (Conway, 2013).

9. 2013-2014: A Belated Recovery

From 2013 onwards, there was a noticeable improvement in the four main economic indicators. The UK economy grew at a rate of 1.9 per cent in 2013, the first year since 2007 without at least one quarter of negative growth (BBC News, 2014a; Rogers & Sedghi, 2013; ONS, 2014). In the three months to February 2014, unemployment fell to its lowest level in five years (BBC News, 2014c). In the same month, the country's trade deficit fell to £7.72 billion, its lowest level since July 2012. Inflation, while falling to its target level of 2 per cent in January 2014, had since proceeded to fall steadily lower, reaching 1.6 per cent in March.

In its March 2014 EFO, the OBR (2014: p.10-11) judged that while unemployment had fallen faster than expected given the improved growth figures, productivity and wage growth remained disappointing.

> Consumer spending, supported by a falling saving ratio, has been the biggest driver of recent growth, while the latest data suggest business investment is recovering. Housing market indicators have picked up sharply, but export performance remains disappointing. (OBR, 2014, p.10)

The OBR had forecast that economic growth would continue in the short term, at a rate of 2.7 per cent in 2014 and at 2.3 per cent in 2015, though that quarter-on-quarter growth would ease as consumption fell in line with household income (Op. cit.). The output gap was estimated at 1.7 per cent and expected to close by approximately mid-2018 (rather than 2013 as it initially forecast), by which time the bulk of the deficit would have been reduced (again, later than originally forecast).

The OBR estimated the budget deficit for the year 2013-14 at £107.8 billion (equivalent to 6.8 per cent of GDP) and for the year 2014-15 at 5.6 per cent of GDP (OBR, 2013: 3). Short term borrowing was expected to fall gradually as a result of stronger receipts and lower spending year-on-year. However:

> exports are all but flat, despite the 20% fall in the value of the pound since the crisis; and manufacturing output remains 9% below where it was in 2008 (Stewart, 2013)

The Governor of the Bank of England Mark Carney stated in January 2014 that though encouraging, the recovery had not yet proved to be sustainable. Monetary policy would, he assured, be likely to remain loose until at least the next general election:

> "A few quarters of above-trend growth driven by household spending are a good start but they aren't sufficient for sustained momentum ... For a sustained and balanced recovery, the degree of stimulus will need to remain exceptional for some time." (Elliott & Monaghan, 2014)

Although there certainly had been a commendable slight advance, economic indicators illustrated little improvement relative to 2010, when the coalition had assumed office and relative to pre-crisis levels. While UK GDP was forecast to return to its pre-crisis peak in 2015, Germany had already recovered to this stage by 2011 and recovery in France had consistently outstripped the UK.

9.1 "Distributional Effects" and the "Cost of Living Crisis"

IMF research showed that, contrary to the view expressed by proponents of austerity, budget cuts do have (significant and lasting) distributional effects.

> On average, episodes of fiscal adjustments are associated with a sizeable increase in income inequality ... In fact, looking at cumulative changes in the share of wage income in GDP before and after the occurrence of a consolidation episode, it seems that, even though on a declining trend, the wage income share has decreased more rapidly after the occurrence of a consolidation episode. (Ball et al, 2013, p.5)

The fundamental reason for fiscal consolidations affecting certain sections of the population more than others was that when public spending is cut, those that depended on the state for part (or all) of their income were directly affected.

> while growth has finally returned after three damaging years of flatlining, millions of people are not feeling any recovery in their own lives and standard of living ... Headline figures often struggle to give us the full picture. Average earnings figures, which can be driven by large pay rises at the top, often mask what is happening in the middle and at the bottom. We know that bankers' pay in London, where most of the top earners are based, grew nearly five times faster than the pay of the average worker last year. (Balls, 2014)

The Shadow Chancellor Ed Balls had been arguing since the return of economic growth in 2013 that for the vast majority, the economic recovery had not led to an increase in living standards – and that this had been the slowest economic recovery for over a century. Relevant ONS data showed that GDP per capita in fact remained (in 2013) at roughly 2004 levels.

the economy was only ½ per cent larger in the first quarter of 2012 as it was in the third quarter of 2010. Indeed, per capita GDP - the simplest measure of the UK's overall economic prosperity - actually fell over this period; we do not expect it to regain its pre-recession peak until approximately 2018. (Portes, 2013c)

This was problematic for the Chancellor George Osborne because in his emergency budget speech he had pledged "an economy where prosperity is shared among all sections of society and all parts of the country" (Osborne, 2010). Among its eight "Benchmarks for Britain", the 2010 Conservative manifesto outlined the Party's pledge to:

> Ensure the whole country shares in rising prosperity: We will increase the private sector's share of the economy in all regions of the country, especially outside London and the South east. (Conservative Party, 2010)

9.2 **The Quantity and Quality of Employment**

The increase in headline employment figures belied the quality of the work available: increasing numbers of people had been forced to accept casual, insecure and low-paying work. The number of workers on "zero hours" contracts – where employers are not obligated to offer any hours – was estimated at around one million by the Chartered Institute of Personnel and Development (CIPD, 2013) with around 14 per cent reporting that their employers offered insufficient hours each week. As Seumas Milne argued:

> The hallmarks of David Cameron's Britain are becoming clearer: payday loans, food banks, the bedroom tax, G4S and now zero-hours contracts ... Agency working, temporary work and enforced part-time working have all mushroomed: nearly half the jobs created since 2008 have been temporary, as half a million permanent jobs have been lost. (Milne, 2013)

While employment had increased steadily in recent years, the number of people in under-employment – those in work seeking but unable to acquire more hours – remained high, such that headline employment figures concealed the true extent of the under-utilisation of resources (Bell & Blanchflower, 2013).

there has been such a dramatic increase in underemployment that the unemployment rate is now a poorer indicator of the degree of slack in the labour market than it has been in the recent past. Further, estimates of the 'output gap' that rely on the unemployment rate may be giving a seriously misleading estimate of the degree of excess capacity in the UK labour market. (Bell & Blanchflower, 2013, p.8)

10. "Britain is Turning a Corner"

"The evidence increasingly suggests that our macroeconomic plan was the right one and is working." (BBC News, 2013)

In September 2013, George Osborne argued that recent economic growth estimates were evidence that the government's economic strategy was working. He had claimed that the adoption of a Plan B involving increased government borrowing would have risked sucking the UK into the European sovereign debt crisis, undermined its ability to follow an activist monetary policy, and undermined its recovery from the Great

Recession. The Chancellor reiterated that budget cuts were necessary in averting the dangers of unsustainable debt and that living standards would be lower in their absence.

> "Proponents of the fiscalist story cannot explain why the UK recovery has strengthened rapidly over the last six months. The pace of fiscal consolidation has not changed, government spending cuts have continued as planned, and yet growth has accelerated" (Wintour, 2013)

The Chancellor defended the government's economic strategy on the basis that budget cuts had not stifled economic growth but rather had contributed to its return. As such, expansionary fiscal consolidation had been successfully implemented, proving the recent research on fiscal multipliers wrong. Jonathan Portes described this view as "an obvious sleight of hand"[12], pointing to the

---

[12] A further "slight of hand" was removed in December 2018 when the reporting of the impact of student debt was changed – as the BBC reported:
> A change in how student loans are recorded in the public finances will add £12bn to the deficit, following an Office

OBR's statement in its March 2013 EFO that deficit reduction had stalled (a view shared by the OECD, the IMF and Mark Carney). Further, the Chancellor maintained that:

> "the composition and timing of the slowdown in GDP growth relative to forecast is better explained by external inflation shocks, the eurozone crisis and the ongoing impact of the financial crisis on financial conditions." (Portes, 2013)

This view however, had been rebuked by the OBR in March 2013, with Robert Chote reiterating that the OBR's forecasts assume, contrary to the government, that fiscal consolidations are a drag on growth. It was likely that its overestimations of growth:

---

for National Statistics ruling. ... Student loans will now significantly push up the UK's deficit - providing an incentive to reduce tuition fees. ...The decision by the statistics agency tackles an anomaly in which the cost of lending to students, to cover fees and maintenance, has been missing from the public finances. It will significantly increase the deficit - which is the difference between what the government spends and what it receives. (BBC, 18th December 2018)

> reflected several factors, including the impact of stubborn inflation on real consumer spending, deteriorating export markets on net trade, and impaired credit conditions, euro area anxiety and demand uncertainty on business investment. Fiscal consolidation may also have done more to slow growth than we assumed. (OBR, 2012, p.8)

In its October 2013 Forecast Evaluation Report, the OBR judged that fiscal multipliers had, as Blanchard and Leigh concluded, been underestimated (meaning that fiscal consolidations were more contractionary during downturns than previously understood).

A further essential difficulty with this view however, was that it was at odds with the literature on expansionary fiscal consolidation. The literature (Giavazzi and Pagano, 1990; Blanchard, 1990; Alesina and Ardagna, 2009) explained that fiscal adjustments might be expansionary through the expectations channel (alternatively, the confidence channel). There was an initial fall in national income resulting from the fiscal adjustment, however, it was argued that this would be counterbalanced indirectly through the effect of budget cuts on expectations.

10.1 The Confidence Effect

Crucially, the literature assumed that consumption was a function of permanent income. As such, the announcement of a credible programme of budget cuts should have been sufficient in signalling a change of regime and as such, there should have been an immediate increase in permanent income and a consequent increase in current consumption, which should lead, through this offsetting of the initial fiscal adjustment, to an increase in national income. However, as the Chancellor himself noted, the recovery in economic growth came in 2013 rather than immediately after the emergency budget speech in 2010. This was not the way in which consolidations are expansionary in the literature; there should not be a lag between the announcement of cuts and the resultant growth materialising as was forecast. The very existence of lags formed part of the rationale opposing expansionary fiscal policy.

Further, the literature itself stated that such expansions hinged upon perfectly functioning credit markets. In their absence, individuals would not be able to increase consumption, even if their permanent incomes had increased following the announcement of cuts – unless they reduced their savings, which the OBR had evaluated as contributing to consumption growth. The Bank of England (2013: p.6) reported that consumer credit remained on its way to returning to pre-crisis levels and that:

> The annual rate of growth in the stock of lending to UK businesses was negative in the three months to August. The stock of lending to small and medium-sized enterprises and to large businesses also contracted over this period. (BoE, 2013, p.3)

As Portes had evaluated, the coalition had eased the pace of fiscal consolidation, with OBR forecasts showing that the rate of deficit reduction had slowed since 2011-12 and would not gather pace until after the next general election. In its October 2013 FER, the OBR documented that:

> the overall consolidation planned by 2015-16 is slightly smaller than planned in June 2010, but with the Government pencilling in additional tightening in 2016-17 and 2017-18, mainly through current spending

cuts. Relative to the plans in June 2010, there is now slightly less additional tightening projected in 2013-14, the same amount in 2014-15 and more in 2015-16, followed up with bigger cuts in the subsequent two years. (OBR, 2013, p.52-53)

The OBR (2013, p.54) judged that fiscal consolidation, especially in latter years, had a greater effect on GDP than was widely understood (and assumed by the OBR itself) in 2010. Fiscal consolidation had been forecast to have resulted in a fall in GDP of over 1 per cent between 2011 and 2016 with the contractionary effect fading from 2013 onwards. Jonathan Portes explained that:

> the bounce back in the level of GDP – and hence the positive impact on growth – simply comes arithmetically from the fact that fiscal consolidation had a significant negative impact on GDP in 2011-12 and 12-13, and those effects are fading out – producing a boost to growth. (Portes, 2013)

Crucially, this meant that the economic recovery from 2013 onwards could be adequately explained by the "fiscalist story" as Osborne described it in his speech. As Simon Wren-Lewis explained:

> In the textbook case austerity implies a deeper recession but then a subsequent recovery that is stronger as a result. So in that case rapid growth provides evidence in *favour* of the "fiscalist" case, not against it. (Wren-Lewis, 2013)

Part Four:

Evaluation of Austerity in the UK

This part of our story evaluates the effects of austerity and scrutinises its original justifications. We will also ask why austerity was persisted with, given that there were the various subsequent contrasting views –

- the OBR's view that fiscal consolidation was necessarily a drag on growth;

- the IMF's view that consolidation should be eased;

- the view of the *The National Institute of Economic and Social Research* (NIESR) that its easing had brought improved growth;

- and the Conservatives' own pronouncements that the purpose of cuts had always been deficit reduction,

We can ask why did George Osborne maintain that the government stance on austerity had been right from the start?

11. Austerity Scrutinised

Queried by John Mann MP at a meeting of the Treasury Select Committee in 2010, George Osborne conceded that the UK national debt as a percentage of GDP was neither at its highest level in history, in Osborne's lifetime, nor higher than Italy, France, Japan or the US.[13] What then, Mann asked, justified the coalition's fiscal mandate? The Chancellor replied that the elimination of the structural budget deficit over a single parliament was necessary in order to demonstrate the credibility of the coalition's fiscal adjustment. However, was the Chancellor right to argue that the UK could have been sucked into the European sovereign debt crisis?

The Shadow Secretary of State for Work and Pensions, Rachel Reeves, pointed out in 2010 that the UK was different to the eurozone member states in a number of crucial respects. Firstly, the UK situation had not been comparable to that of Greece because:

> not only does Greece have a higher level of debt, but it has more pressure to continually refinance

---

[13] Ensuing IMF data showed that the UK national debt had remained lower against these comparators in 2014.

that debt. The Financial Times puts the average UK debt maturity at 13.5 years, which compares with 7.9 years for Greece, 6.4 years for Spain, and 5.4 years for Ireland. A March 2010 Financial Times article noted that "the UK is a stark outlier: the average maturity of the gilt market is currently 14 years, longer than almost anywhere else in the world." (Reeves, 2010)

Secondly, the UK had not been part of a currency union and as such, had a greater deal of flexibility over monetary policy. This meant that short term interest rates could be tailored with specific goals in mind, whether these were a given inflation rate or unemployment level – as the Bank of England had done. Finally, while the majority of Greek debt was held internationally, making it vulnerable to global markets, 80% of British sovereign debt had been held by British institutions and individuals, as explained by Paul Segal (2010).

> We put our savings in banks and pensions funds. But they are just intermediaries: they invest our savings by buying bonds and other securities that pay interest. Some of these bonds will be from private

> sector companies that want to borrow for investment. But when private companies do not want to invest as much as we ... want to save in a given year, then the only alternative is to invest the money in government bonds ... The fiscal deficit is so high because we are demanding more bonds – that is, we want to save more – than the private sector is willing to invest. (Segal, 2010)

The magnitude of the budget deficit therefore, was not necessarily problematic, but rather a reflection of the business cycle: the private sector was choosing to lend to the government as it was a relatively safe investment in the then current economic environment. A high level of deficit expenditure, especially in the case of the UK, was a reflection of the high demand for sovereign bonds. It was for these reasons that Andrew Tyrie, Chair of the Treasury Select Committee:

> said Osborne's claim that Britain had been "on the brink of bankruptcy" was "a bit over the top". He also challenged the chancellor's claims that his emergency budget had been progressive, accusing him

of "over-egging it a bit". (Inman, 2010)

The national debt was not especially high in historical terms either. In fact, in 1948, the UK's debt-to-GDP ratio stood at almost three times current levels, yet under the administration of Clement Attlee, in that year, the National Health Service Act (1946) and the National Assistance Act (1948) had come into effect, establishing nationalised healthcare free at the point of use and a social safety net for those who did not pay national insurance contributions. Howard Reed and Thomas Clark (R&C) (2013) recalled that:

> Before 2008, an avowedly modernising Conservative party committed to match Labour's public spending totals. However, two weeks after Lehman Brothers went bust in 2008, George Osborne took to the rostrum at his party's conference and reverted to Tory type, sternly announcing that "borrowing is out of control" ... the early stirrings of a debt crisis in southern Europe lent superficial credibility to fears that Britain was teetering on bankruptcy. (Reed & Clark, 2013)

Reed and Clark illustrated that curiously enough, the UK's debt-to-GDP ratio had in fact stood at around 80 per cent for much of the past 300 years; the low debt-to-GDP of the latter half of the last century was, as such, an aberration.

> If Britain is broke at the moment, then the graph shows that it was also broke for a whole century between 1750 and 1850, and for 20 years after the second world war. In reality, in neither case did the UK default, and reveal itself as bust – both periods were times of investment, growth and national renewal. (Ibid.)

Although Alesina (2010, p.2) argued that the 1980s and 1990s represented a better comparison to the current period than the inter-war period or the 1950s, this was itself a normative statement. The nationalisations and fiscal stimulus of the Attlee administration show that there was no single, universal instruction sheet for economic policy. Ultimately, as with all policies, austerity was a choice based on values, ideology, circumstances and a myriad of other factors. Crucially, Osborne, by his own admission, was not forced to reduce expenditure but targeted the elimination of the structural deficit on his own evaluation and at his own instigation.

11.1 **Was the Fiscal Mandate Realistic?**

Will Hutton warned in 2010 that the coalition's planned fiscal adjustment was without precedent. This was the largest voluntary fiscal consolidation and importantly, conducted on different circumstances to previous overseas adjustments.

> The former Labour government had already committed to a greater and faster reduction in the budget deficit than any British government in modern times. The coalition government wants to do more; to nearly eliminate a structural budget deficit of 8% of national output – some £116bn – in five years. Moreover, it wants spending cuts to take 80% of the load. No country has ever volunteered such austerity. It is as tough a package of retrenchment as the IMF imposed on Greece, a country on the brink of bankruptcy. It is twice as tough as the famously harsh measures Canada took between 1994 and 1997. It is three times tougher than

Sweden's measures between 1993 and 1995. In British terms, it is immeasurably tougher than what we did after the IMF crisis in 1976 or after the ERM crisis in 1992.

Sweden took 15 years to lower some departmental spending by 20%, not the five years the government plans. We are not in the position of Greece. Britain has a diversified economy. Our cumulative national debt is not large by international standards. Uniquely, the term structure of our debt is very long – around 14 years. Most of this year's debt will be sold to British domiciled individuals and companies, so the international sovereign debt crisis has much less impact on us. The level of interest on the national debt in five years' time as a share of national output is more than manageable. These are the truths about the situation; to claim otherwise creates distrust. (Hutton, 2010)

11.2 How Necessary was Austerity?

Richard Drayton further explained why austerity was not an economic necessity but rather a policy choice favourable to

Conservative and Liberal Democrat voters. The costs of servicing debt had in recent years been exceptionally low.

> What is clear is that in May 2010 the percentage of UK GDP which went to servicing debt, even after the impact of the 2008 crisis, was, at 2.5 per cent, at the lowest level enjoyed by any Conservative government since Lord Salisbury was at the Treasury in 1900. By no metric in 2010 was the present or projected debt burden of the UK in historical terms very high, let alone unsustainable.

> "Austerity" today is being used deliberately, across the board, to justify the acceleration of this transfer of public services into private hands ... The price of austerity will be a long-term decline in the standard of living of the majority of the population, and an acceleration of the now thirty-year-long experiment in transferring wealth from the poor and middle classes to the richest. By this measure ... a powerful minority might consider this success rather than "failure". (Drayton, 2013)

There were of course, as many alternatives to austerity as there are ways to adjust government budgets. The lack of support for these measures may be best explained by the orthodoxy within the economics profession, or the influence of the corporate and financial sectors on government. Mark Blyth (2013) has argued the former view, Simon Johnson and James Kwak (2011) the latter.

A financial transactions tax – or a Tobin tax after James Tobin, who proposed the levy in 1972 – represents the most equitable, though perhaps least feasible alternative to austerity. Its central principle is just: revenues from financial transactions should form the basis of bank bailouts.

> Tobin said it had to be an internationally agreed uniform tax to work effectively. He said each government would levy it with the proceeds paid into a global financial body such as the World Bank or the International Monetary Fund (IMF). Tobin suggested a rate of 0.5%, but other economists have put forward rates ranging from 0.1% to 1%. Even at a very low rate, supporters argue that if it were imposed on all financial transactions across the

world, it could raise billions of pounds. (BBC News, 2013)

The size of the financial sector in the UK made it feasible as a means of revenue generation if there was the political will to enforce it – which arguably there should have been given the relish with which the coalition, and the G20, had insisted upon budget cuts, particularly in welfare expenditure.

Though the tax was implemented unsuccessfully in Sweden, where a fraction of the expected revenues were raised ultimately – in this regard it was essentially no different to austerity, which despite generalised disappointing results had been maintained through political will.

11.3 Fiscal Consolidation and "Distributional Effects"

Initially, widespread public anger followed banking sector bailouts as it was perceived that bankers, those responsible for the financial crisis, had seen their failure subsidised by the taxpayer. This popular opposition had continued to build up over recent years as the measures implemented to reduce the structural deficit have been heavily weighted in favour of expenditure cuts rather than (progressive) taxation increases. Former Governor of the Bank of England Mervyn King admitted at a meeting of the Treasury select Committee in 2011 that:

> "The price of this financial crisis is being borne by people who absolutely did not cause it," he said. (Inman, 2011)

Widespread public anger was perhaps best understood in the context that in post-war Britain, it had become commonplace to believe it was a role of the state to finance the basic social safety net in place since the Clement Atlee administration. From the 1970s onwards, this role has increasingly been challenged by market libertarians and neoliberals, who argued that – despite the Great Depression and the Great Recession – the market, intrinsically, had an unrivalled capacity for efficiency and self-regulation, such that it may be even entrusted with the provision of what had historically been conceived of as public or merit goods (those which are intrinsically undervalued under a market mechanism).

11.4 The Paradox of Thrift and the Balance Sheet Recession

Anatole Kaletsky (2013) noted that the government's launch of *Help to Buy* in 2013 is a tacit acceptance of the need for stimulus rather than austerity; that:

> Britain has finally been forced to accept Keynes's "paradox of thrift". A government that tries to reduce its borrowing during a recession generally weakens the economy so much that it ends up increasing its total debt. Conversely, a government that expands deficits during periods of weak economic activity, or finds ways to encourage private borrowing and discourage private saving, usually ends up lightening the national debt burden.
>
> Instead of trying to reduce borrowing any further or aiming for a balanced budget, as it originally promised, the British government has now accepted that deficits will keep rising in absolute terms and will still be worth 6% of GDP by the next election in 2015. That would leave Britain with by far the highest deficit ratio among the major economies after five years of unprecedented austerity.

> Meanwhile the U.S., with comparatively little fiscal effort, is projected to reduce its deficit to just 2.4% by 2015. (Kaletsky, 2013)

Ultimately, proponents of austerity based their analysis on the economy at its full employment level. This adequately explains the insistence that fiscal multipliers are low and that individuals may increase their consumption following budget cuts. However, this analysis was being misapplied in the current period, whereas the OBR continued to recognise, spare capacity remained in the economy, and would do so until around 2018; unemployment still had a long way to go before it returned to its pre-crisis level, as did GDP. Economic policy should be tailored to the business cycle, however, much of the intellectual foundations of austerity measures refuted the very existence of a protracted business cycle. The notion of a structural budget deficit itself was predicated upon the notion of a natural rate of unemployment; that where there exists equilibrium in the labour market, unemployment is voluntary.

Since 2010 the private sectors in the U.S., the U.K., Spain, and Ireland (but less so Greece) have undergone significant deleveraging in spite of record low interest rates. This means these countries are all in serious balance sheet recessions. The private sectors in Japan and Germany are not borrowing, either. With borrowers disappearing and banks reluctant to lend, it is no wonder that, after many years of record low interest rates and massive liquidity injections, industrial economies are still doing so poorly. (Koo, 2012)

11.5 How Did the UK's National Debt Proliferate?

Contrary to the coalition view that the Labour Party was profligate in government, Howard Reed (2012) disclosed that under the Blair and Brown administrations, government consumption was only marginally higher than during the Major administration and actually lower than under the Thatcher administration. Further, under Labour, government investment was also lower.

As previously explained in Section 1, national debt proliferated as a result of state bailouts and deficit expenditure in the wake of the 2007-08 financial crisis, without which, it is worth recalling, the ensuing recession may have been considerably more damaging (IMF, 2013, p.4: OECD, 2012: Blyth, 2013).

> The economic crisis that began in 2008 caused government deficits to surge, and fiscal imbalances were swollen further by stimulus measures and bank rescue operations. Together, these forces led to ballooning public indebtedness, the general government public debt-GDP ratio rising from under 80% of GDP in 2008 to almost 100% of GDP in 2011 (OECD, 2012, p.3)

The financial crisis itself resulted directly from private sector actions, which though rational and optimal on a microeconomic scale, presented massive systemic risks. While it may have been safe for individuals to lever up significantly, the result of high leverage *en masse* was a long boom and the protracted slump that has now been experienced. This much was recognised in the letter sent to HM the Queen on behalf of the British Academy in 2009.

> Everyone seemed to be doing their own job properly on its own merit. And according to standard measures of success, they were often doing it well. The failure was to see how collectively this added up to a series of interconnected imbalances over which no single

> authority had jurisdiction. This, combined with the psychology of herding and the mantra of financial and policy gurus, lead to a dangerous recipe. Individual risks may rightly have been viewed as small, but the risk to the system as a whole was vast. (Besley & Hennessy, 2009, p.3)

The causes of the 2007-08 financial crisis and the disappointing performance of austerity measures in its wake, taken together, support the Keynesian paradigm. The appeasement of the financial markets, if it were necessary (in the UK it is not as most of the national debt is held domestically), could not prevent another financial crisis. The coalition therefore, either held a mistaken view regarding the causes of the crisis and the capacity for austerity to be successful – or had implemented austerity for other reasons altogether.

11.6 Austerity in a Downturn

In February 2014, the Manchester Evening News reported that Greater Manchester taxpayers are spending £1.6 billion more on welfare expenditure and public services than five years ago.

> Sir Richard Leese, leader of Manchester council, said: "Since this government has been in power expenditure hasn't gone down, it has actually moved from services, especially local authority services, to greater benefit expenditure and expenditure on health." (Linton, 2014)

Austerity implemented during a downturn is especially myopic, as recent research has shown (see Section 8 above). This should not be a surprise unless one starts from neoclassical assumptions, though even then, the permanent income hypothesis states clearly its contingency upon well-functioning credit markets. During a period of higher than normal unemployment, imperfect access to credit and still-recovering aggregate demand, austerity will inevitably result in increased dependence on the state.

This dependence on the part of the public becomes a problem when it coincides with demands from failing banks which have in recent years taken priority, to the ire of much of the general public, which feel, perhaps with much justification, that the massive bank bailouts represented a betrayal of the principles of capitalism.

This leads to perhaps the most common critique of neoliberalism – that it invariably results in the privatisation of gains and the socialisation of losses. This view, expressed vehemently by Nassim Nicholas Taleb, was the most obvious interpretation of the policy response to the 2007-08 financial crisis and to a large extent is not without merit.

> This is a free option. The risk is borne by ... you and I, the taxpayers. We take the downside and Wall Street, as usual, is going to take the upside. It's another classical problem of what I call socialising the losses; privatising the gains. (Taleb, 2009).

12. Austerity and Ideology

Early in 2014, Osborne had accepted that the economic recovery remained too reliant on consumption, although he maintained that the government's economic strategy was appropriate.

> "Some in Britain might be tempted to say, "job done – let's avoid more hard decisions" ... That would be a huge mistake. Abandon the plan and we abandon the progress we've made and go back to square one ...

> we have to go on dealing with our debt and our deficit - and we have no choice but to do so ... we cannot put all our chips on the success of the City of London, as my predecessors did" (BBC News, 2014)

This line of argument expressed a deep conviction in the supremacy of the market economy. The thought underpinning it shares a great deal with the Austrian view that the market is the purest expression of human action – with natural and evolutionary properties that the state is incapable of matching – as well as the neoclassical view that the business cycle results from exogenous disturbances. In this view, the market must be left to its own devices in order to function efficiently. In April 2013, when Fitch became the second of the three major rating agencies to downgrade the UK's credit rating, George Osborne's response was to reiterate his original position.

> This is a stark reminder that the UK cannot simply run away from its problems, or refuse to deal with a legacy of debt built up over a decade. (BBC News, 2013c)

When the IMF updated its position on the effects of fiscal consolidation during a downturn, its view was irrelevant, because in the New Keynesian, Austrian and classically liberal thought underpinning the position of the Conservatives, there is no meaningful multiplier effect and expansionary fiscal policy is countervailed by Ricardian equivalence. This view however, was dogmatic and rendered austerity unfalsifiable. The 2007-08 financial crisis showed as clearly as possible the consequences of deregulated and "efficient" markets. Financial markets, when they are permitted the sovereignty argued for by market partisans, failed with enormous systemic and social repercussions. In January 2014, the then Deputy Prime Minister Nick Clegg distanced himself from the Conservative Party, stating that:

> "You've got a Conservative party now who are driven, it seems to me, by two very clear ideological impulses. One is to remorselessly pare back the state – for ideological reasons just cut back the state.
>
> "Secondly – and I think they are making a monumental mistake in doing so – they say the only people in society, the only section in

> society, which will bear the burden of further fiscal consolidation are the working-age poor." (Watt & Mason, 2014)

Vince Cable, the then Secretary of State for Business, Innovation and Skills, accepted the Conservative view that there was a real danger of the UK public finances deteriorating to the point where investors lost confidence, though predicated austerity on this pragmatic basis alone.

> "Undoubtedly some on the Conservative side of the coalition see fiscal consolidation as a cover for an ideologically driven "small state" agenda. Indeed, it is one thing to respond to a record deficit after a long period of rising public spending, as we have since 2010. It is quite another to continue cutting hard from a position where the debt burden is falling and when spending has been under pressure for half a decade." (Elliott, 2014b)

The Conservatives' insistence to continue with, and refusal to ease the pace of, fiscal consolidation is also at odds with its own pronouncements. In his emergency budget speech in 2010,

Osborne stated that fiscal consolidation was based on a consensus formed at the Toronto summit of the G20. In his 2010 New Year message, David Cameron stated that:

> "We're tackling the deficit because we have to – not out of some ideological zeal. This is a government led by people with a practical desire to sort out this country's problems, not by ideology." (Eaton, 2010)

Osborne's insistence in September 2013 that the pace of cuts had not been eased, and remained appropriate, however, was at odds with the consensus position of the G20 following the Mexico City summit in June 2012, that fiscal consolidation should be flexible (Thomson, 2012).

12.1 **Austerity and Neoliberalism**

A strong case can be made that the turn to austerity only makes sense if it considered as part of the evolution of capitalism and the balance of class power within it — towards wealthy households, economically dominant firms (chief among them being financial firms), conservative politicians and right-wing populists. (King et al, 2012, p.3)

One of the consequences of high public debt is that it becomes a justification for almost any form of budget cuts; even essential public services are not exempt. Consequently, it has become commonplace to understand all activities as fundamentally private and individualistic, rather than fundamentally rooted in society, solidarity or national identity.

In the neoliberal view, public services are not necessarily special and in recent decades, many state-owned enterprises have been sold or part-privatised. In the current climate, the NHS, arguably the most essential public service of all, remains under threat.

The nature of neoliberalism, as such, is puzzling. In the name of increased competition and efficiency, nationalised services and industries have been privatised time and again. In the case of rail travel massive public subsidies are still required. Banking deregulation in the 1980s and light-touch regulation under the previous Labour government infamously led to the greatest financial crisis in generations. Most members of the Cabinet held directorships alongside their front bench duties and many, such as Sajid Javid, who replaced Maria Miller as Secretary of State for Culture, have had careers in banking and finance. As John Gray explains:

Neoliberals wanted to limit government, but the upshot of their policies has been a huge expansion in the power of the state ... Shrinking the state has proved politically impossible, so neoliberals have turned instead to using the state to reshape social institutions on the model of the market - a task that cannot be carried out by a small state ... If there is no reason in theory why the neoliberal state must develop in a social-democratic direction, neither is there any reason in practice. A more likely course of events is that social democracy will be eroded even further. (Gray, 2010)

12.2. **Austerity and Financialisation**

Austerity, on balance, has cemented, if not furthered financialisation. The approximate doubling of the national debt that resulted from the 2007-08 financial crisis enabled the implementation of liberal economic policies in such a way as to shift economic and political power from the real sector and individuals towards the financial sector and financial elites.

One of the defining characteristics of the 2007-08 crisis and its aftermath was the extent to which financialisation entrenched itself. This is especially remarkable in that what has become known as the Great Recession has been the most severe economic crisis in almost a century. UK GDP still has not returned to its pre-crisis peak.

It did not take long from the onset of stagflation in the 1970s for neoliberal ideas to become part of conventional thinking. In contrast, while the recent crisis saw a brief return to Keynesianism, the turn to austerity marked a return to neoliberal orthodoxy, as noted by King et al (2012).

A curious contradiction lies at the heart of neoliberal thought. As market deregulation, privatisation and liberalisation has increased, financial crises have become increasingly common and severe – despite neoclassical and New Keynesian economics insisting that exogenous factors are the cause of business cycles. Despite this proposition, the state has increasingly been relied upon to bailout failed financial institutions and markets.

However, the same assistance has increasingly been denied to the vast majority of the general public. On the one hand, insurance for banks is essential, on the other, insurance for the general public is unaffordable. This contradiction was, as Blyth (2013) noted, inequitable and the main reason why austerity was more than a "purely economic" phenomenon. Neoliberalism has not resulted in a greater emphasis on market incentives and freer markets but rather the socialisation of financial sector losses along with the privatisation of its gains. This was epitomised by the urgency with which the coalition government sought to re-privatise RBS and Lloyds TSB, even at the risk of selling the taxpayer's shares in the banks at a loss.

> Parallel to its capturing of the academy, the financial industry's money has co-opted much of the US political elite in both parties ... between 1999 and 2009 the financial industry spent $3.5 billion on lobbying and $2.2 billion on campaign donations. (King et al, 2012, p.2)

There has been a comprehensive capture of public institutions over the past four decades to the extent that public life is becoming increasingly neoliberal in nature. There has been the cultivation of an antidemocratic consensus that elevates financial interests above all else. This is epitomised by the emergency IMF lending to Italy and Greece that came subject to the governmental appointments of Mario Monti and Lucas Papademos (both former Goldman Sachs bankers). Closer to home:

> Ed Balls says he will seek to run a budget surplus in the next parliament if Labour wins the next election as it would be the "right thing to do". The shadow chancellor said a surplus would be an aspiration, but he could not promise that it would happen before 2020 because it depended on the health of the economy. (Mason, 2013)

Both sides of the political mainstream have been gripped by an irrational fear of the stability of public finances when the preponderance of research shows to the contrary that the imbalances at the root of the recent crisis were in the private sector – as are the imbalances likely to be at the root of the next economic crisis. In its March 2013 Quarterly Bulletin, the Bank of England (BoE) warned that the dramatic increase in leveraged takeovers by private equity firms in the 2000s may present a systemic risk in the coming years as the:

> resulting increase in indebtedness makes those companies more susceptible to default, exposing their lenders to potential losses. This risk is compounded by the need for companies to refinance a cluster of buyout debt maturing over the next few years in an environment of much tighter credit conditions. (BoE, 2013a, p.38)

Fundamental theoretical questions were not engaged with by those in positions of influence as they were in the aftermath of the Great Inflation of the 1970s and as a result, it would seem on the surface that the 2007-08 financial crisis has gone to waste, so to speak.

> The policy lesson learned by the most powerful (and solvent) European state was that policy failures by governments, not financial markets, make crises. Consequently, the policy "success" of 2008 – the return of the master and his stimulus measures – was seen by the Germans and their allies at the ECB as a policy disaster waiting to happen whose consequences would only become all too apparent in future inflation. (Blyth, 2013, p.55-56)

Expansionary austerity has been championed on the basis of political and ideological rather than scientific or academic merit. The IMF itself stated that the conventional approach to identifying cases of fiscal consolidation (as in the research conducted by Alesina and Ardagna) "is far from perfect and can bias the results toward finding expansionary effects" (IMF, 2010, p.95-96).

12.3 **Austerity, Wages and profits**

If one believes the so-called *Iron Law of Wages*, then workers' wages will be held down, by competition, to a subsistence level.

> The Natural Price of labour is that price which is necessary to enable the labourers, one with another, to subsist and to perpetuate their race, without either increase or diminution. (Ricardo, I, p.93)

However, Ricardo realised that this basis level was indeed a socially necessary or defined subsistence level:

> It is not to be understood that the natural price of labour, estimated

> even in food and necessaries, is absolutely fixed and constant. It varies at different times in the same country, and very materially in different times in different countries. It essentially depends on the habits and customs of the people. (ibid, p.97)

Thereby, wages have an inverse relationship with profits, or Profits equating to the residual remaining after wages and rent have been paid out of the revenue received for goods sold.

> can any point be more clearly established than that profits must fall, with a rise of wages? ... for nothing can affect profits but arise in wages: (ibid, p.115, 118)

Thus, real wage increases result in decreased profits and visa versa. Thereby, Austerity, by lowering the socially acceptable subsistence level, i.e. real wages, will have the effect of raising profits.

Austerity thus becomes a means to counteract the falling rate of profits tendency, and thus a necessary or desirable policy for conservative economics.

13. Austerity's Impact Upon Society

In line with our previous discussions in sections 2.3 and 2.5, along with footnote No. 9, Austerity can be seen as another attempt to further embedded Society into the Economy.

For example, education used to be embedded within society, it was primarily a social or community concern. However, now, perhaps with added impetus derived from financialisation, education is being disembedded (or disconnected) from society and embedded into the economy. The new school Academies are operated as business, rather than social institutions, and a similar transformation can be seen with British Universities. Education has ceased being so much a social issue but is increasingly being directed by and delivered for economic (i.e. profit) purposes.

As such, the economy initially disembedded itself from society so that, as an inevitable alternative, society and its social issues could subsequently become increasingly embedded in the economy.

Austerity can or should be conceived as one of the processes that facilitates such a great transformation.

A major political purpose of austerity has thus been to increasingly subsume society to economic forces, whilst at the same time liberating economic activities from social considerations.

13.1 **The Orange Book and the Big Society**

Both coalition member parties began to emphasise a greater civic and economic role for personal liberty and responsibility. *The Orange Book* reasserted the liberal element within the Liberal Democrat Party and is widely attributed with paving the way for a coalition with the Conservatives (Laws, 2012, p.31). The Conservative Party itself launched a similar initiative, the *Big Society*, with a mission to "put more power and opportunity into people's hands" (Cabinet Office, 2010).

This emphasis on personal responsibility extends to the present day, with the Conservative government still emphasising that they are "for hardworking people". What makes this stance significant is its juxtaposition with the government's stance on commercial and corporate responsibility.

In September 2013, George Osborne filed a lawsuit at the European Court of

Justice against an EU cap on bankers' bonuses (Barker et al, 2013). In a landmark ruling in October 2013, the UK Supreme Court dismissed the Department for Work and Pensions' appeal against the judgement of the Court of Appeal that the government's *Back to Work* schemes were unlawful and should be quashed (Public Interest Lawyers, 2013). That government, while pledging banking reform and a reduction in youth unemployment, had tightened access to benefits for the unemployed and defended the very practices it argued must change. This was in contrast to events in Iceland, where nine senior staff at Kaupthing, one of the country's largest banks, have been criminally charged for market manipulation (Bowers, 2013).[14]

> These cases reflect one of the hallmarks of the coalition's administration: the shift in political representation away from its people to its corporate and financial interests. Despite the stated aims of reducing the size of the state and its burden on current and future

---

[14] The Kaupthing Bank was eventually nationalised and superseded in 2009, by the new Arion Bank.

generations of taxpayers, the state is meaningfully smaller in size, though its policies and actions show that many of its core functions have been transformed. As such, the coalition's administration amounts more to an entrenchment of financialisation rather than a shift towards a new economic model.

13.2 **Austerity and Healthcare**

There was and to a very large extent, currently still is, an ongoing debate concerning the possible privatisation or further marketisation of the NHS in the name of increased efficiency. Ultimately, it is argued, increasing healthcare costs must be remedied through market forces.

Lord Warner (2014) argued that in its then present form, the NHS was imperilled by financial and service inefficiencies. Given the necessity of deficit reduction, and its annual shortfall of around £30 billion, the nation had a choice between NHS reform or "starving other vital public services". New funding streams were required, which Warner argued should involve a monthly fee and (or) the sale or exploitation of the system's fixed assets.

> A new integrated "National Health and Care Service" would pioneer a "co-producing" health partnership between state and citizen, with annual personal health MOTs agreeing responsibilities over the year for both services and the individual. At the heart of this relationship would be an NHS membership scheme, charging £10 a month (with some exemptions) collected through council tax for local preventative services to help people stay healthy. (Warner, 2014).

Lord Warner, however, did not explain how a marketised NHS would deliver greater efficiency. The marketisation of healthcare is potentially only the beginning of a process that leads to its privatisation. Healthcare in the United States, perhaps the UK's closest ally and an important trading partner, however, is more expensive and as a result less accessible to those on low incomes.

> The US has the highest health spending in the world – equivalent to 17.9% of its gross domestic product (GDP), or $8,362 per person. And it's not all private – government spending is at $4,437 per person, only behind

Luxembourg, Monaco and Norway (Rogers, 2012)

It is worth considering that a possible privatisation of the NHS may yet follow the experiences of rail privatisation, which has led not to an increase in efficiency but rather the opposite. Two decades on from privatisation, the Rail Value for Money Study (2011, p.5), led by Sir Roy McNulty, found that in 2008-09, GB Rail should have cost 20-30 per cent less than it did, as well as identifying a 40 per cent efficiency gap as against four European comparators.

The Centre for Research on Socio-Cultural Change (Cresc) found that in 2012, train operating companies earned an average return on investment of 147 per cent (almost one and a half times the capital they spent). This profit, however, rather than being reinvested in the railways, as it was argued would happen, was paid to shareholders; the necessary investment in infrastructure comes at the cost of state subsidies, instead (Chakraborrty, 2013).

13.3 **Austerity and Justice**

In March 2014, thousands of lawyers staged their second walkout of the year in protest against what the Criminal Bar Association described as "crippling" cuts to legal aid (BBC News, 2014e). The aim of the cuts was a £220 million reduction in barristers' and solicitors' fees from the £2 billion annual expenditure on legal aid. Dexter Dias, QC, reproached that the cuts 'simultaneously threaten access to justice, the quality of the representation, and the proper defence of people's rights' (Dias, 2014). The benefits of saving a tenth of the legal aid have then, come at the cost of reducing access to justice.

14 **Concluding Remarks**

In 2010, the coalition government argued that budget cuts were not simply necessary in order to avoid being sucked into the European sovereign debt crisis but that cuts would lead to growth. Throughout the coalition's existence, its conservative members, in particular, have insisted that austerity was right and proper, and urged the public to be patient. In 2013, a belated recovery emerged, which was widely forecast to continue beyond the near term.

The government however, has been assessed by the OBR as unable to deliver on its primary target, the fiscal mandate, as well as its supplementary target. While GDP was expected to recover to its pre-crisis peak, GDP per capita remained at around 2004 levels and this remains the slowest recovery for over a century.

Fiscal consolidation has been thrust upon the country at a time when its people and businesses have been least able to cope with a reduction in the public sector. Burdens on the state have not been reduced but magnified. Wage compression has continued alongside the growth in households reliant on food banks for basic supplies. Widening inequality means that state subsidisation of low wages will have to continue, despite the long-term trend of falling tax receipts compromising this increasingly vital role of the state.

Austerity has led to a reduction in the coverage of essential services such as Legal Aid and increased restrictions on welfare payments at a time when individuals have been least able to cope. Further, initial steps have been taken towards the privatisation of the NHS. As such, whether or not the next government eliminated the structural budget deficit by

2018-19 was irrelevant. The prioritisation of deficit reduction above the provision of public services has, in the final analysis, been the result not of economic necessity, but political and economic ideology.

Appendix I

The 2010 Mais Lecture
- A New Economic Model

Speech by George Osbourne on 24th Feb 2010[15]

Thank you for inviting me to give this annual Mais lecture. Few Mais lectures have been given at a time when the challenges facing British economic policy makers were so difficult and complex as they are today.

Britain has emerged - just - from the longest and deepest recession in living memory, but growth is proving painfully slow to return.

The overhang of private debt in our banking system and our households weighs heavy on future prosperity.

And the public finances are the worst they have ever been in peacetime, with the largest budget deficit in the developed world.

This lecture is about these present problems and the urgent need to take us

---

[15] https://conservative-speeches.sayit.mysociety.org/speech/601526

into a brighter future. But consider this one stark fact about our recent past.

We are coming to the end of the first full Parliament since the Second World War when national income per person has actually declined.

Even through the dark days of the 1970s and the recessions of the early 1980s and 1990s, every full Parliament saw our GDP per capita grow.

But not this Parliament.

When people ask the famous question – "are you better off than you were five years ago?" - this will be the first election in modern British history when the answer from the government must be "no".

My argument today is simple.

Britain has been failed by the economic policy framework of the last decade.

It promised stability, prudence and an end to the cycle - it delivered instability, imprudence and the biggest boom followed by the deepest bust.

We need to head in a completely new direction.

We have to move away from an economic model that was based on unsustainable private and public debt.

And we have to move to a new model of economic growth that is rooted in more investment, more savings and higher exports.

This will require new policies and new institutions.

I want to talk about three crucial components of this new model.

First, a new approach to macroeconomic and financial policy, where we seek to contain credit cycles as well as target price stability.

Second, a new fiscal policy framework, with an independent Office for Budget Responsibility to ensure that public debt is sustainable.

And third, a supply side revolution that releases the pent-up enterprise and wealth creation of our country, encourages a nation of savers, and addresses the long term structural weaknesses that no government has ever properly tackled - like poor education and a welfare system that traps people in workless poverty.

In order to ensure that a Conservative Government is accountable, I have set out eight clear benchmarks for economic policy against which I expect to be judged, together with the concrete measures we will take to achieve them.

If they are met over a Parliament then we will have begun to build a new British economic model.

I also want to explain today why starting to build this new economic model is not something we can put off until next year.

We have to get on with it.

There is no choice between going for growth today and dealing with our debts tomorrow.

Indeed, we will not have any meaningful growth unless we show we can deal with our debts.

For it is the lack of a credible plan to deal with the deficit that is already pushing up market interest rates, undermining the monetary stimulus that

is supporting the economy, and sapping the confidence of investors and consumers.

It is the lack of a credible plan that has the credit rating agencies threatening to downgrade us unless action is taken urgently.

This is the reality of the situation we are facing.

Those who say we should simply ignore the markets are siren voices, luring us onto the rocks.

For an economic policy maker to rail against the unpredictable nature of financial markets is like a farmer complaining about the weather.

A loss of market confidence could force dramatic tax rises and spending cuts that were indeed savage and swingeing.

That would represent a loss of economic sovereignty.

And those cuts would be far larger than the actions that are needed now in order to retain our economic freedom in the first place.

Far better to be prepared and protect ourselves against the storm.

The Dangers of Debt

Before I set out the shape of this new economic model, let us first understand the nature of that storm.

No one doubts that there were massive failures of financial regulation over the last decade.

No one seriously defends the fiscal rules, once spelt out in a Mais Lecture like this, which proved unable to prevent the

Government running a budget deficit at the peak of the boom.

But we will not draw all the right lessons for the future unless we understand the deep macroeconomic roots of the crisis.

Much has already been written about what went wrong. Much more is yet to be written.

Perhaps the most significant contribution to our understanding of the origins of the crisis has been made by Professor Ken Rogoff, former Chief Economist at the IMF, and his co-author Carmen Reinhart.

In a series of papers and now a book, they have demonstrated in exhaustive historical and statistical detail that while it always seems in the heat of the crisis that 'this time is different', the truth is that it almost never is.

As Rogoff and Reinhart demonstrate convincingly, all financial crises ultimately have their origins in one thing - rapid and unsustainable increases in debt.

As they write, "if there is one common theme... it is that excessive debt accumulation, whether it be by the government, banks, corporations, or consumers, often poses greater systemic risks that it seems during a boom."

So, while the specific financial innovations and failures of regulation that contributed to the credit crunch were new, the underlying macroeconomic warning signs were depressingly familiar from many dozens of crises in the past.

In this context, all the signals were flashing red for the UK economy: a rapid increase in household and bank balance sheets, soaring asset prices, a persistent current account deficit, and a structural budget deficit even at the peak of the boom.

Our banks became more leveraged than American banks, and our households became more indebted than any other major economy in history.

And in the aftermath of the crisis our public debt has risen more rapidly than any other major economy.

So, while private sector debt was the cause of this crisis, public sector debt is likely to be the cause of the next one.

As Ken Rogoff himself puts it, "there's no question that the most significant vulnerability as we emerge from recession is the soaring government debt. It's very likely that will trigger the next crisis as governments have been stretched so wide."

The latest research suggests that once debt reaches more than about 90% of GDP the risks of a large negative impact on long term growth become highly significant.

If off-balance sheet liabilities such as public sector pensions are included, we are already well beyond that.

And even on official internationally comparable measures of debt, we are forecast to break through 90% of GDP in just two years' time.

Indeed, baseline projections produced this month from the Bank for International Settlements show the scale of the adjustment that is needed to avoid that risk.

Once the costs of an ageing population are accounted for, they calculate that UK debt will rise to 200% of GDP in just 10 years without significant adjustments - that's higher than any other country except Japan.

The interest payments on that debt would rise above 10% of GDP within ten years and to almost 30% in 30 years - the highest of all the countries they analyse including Greece and Ireland.

The BIS were amongst the few organizations who can credibly claim to have warned about the risks of a global financial crisis, and now they are highlighting the next source of risk.

As they argue, "persistently high levels of public debt will drive down capital accumulation, productivity growth and long-term potential growth potential."

In the short term, governments should not be "lulled into complacency by the ease with which they have financed their deficits so far" - especially those with relatively weak fiscal frameworks and a high degree of dependence on foreign investors.

For an economy like the UK with such high levels of private debt, increases in market interest rates would be particularly devastating to the prospects of a private sector recovery.

We have been warned.

Monetary and Financial Policy

The long-term implications for our economic policy framework of the crucial role of rapid debt accumulation in causing economic instability are profound.

It forces a fundamental reassessment of the way we conduct both monetary and fiscal policy.

Let me begin with monetary policy.

In his famous Mais Lecture of 1984, Nigel Lawson argued that monetary policy should be the main tool of short-term macroeconomic management while fiscal policy should be set for the medium term.

Over time that became the consensus, and it was later explicitly endorsed by the Labour Government.

The monetary policy framework developed too, from the adoption of inflation targeting by the Conservatives in 1992 to the granting of independence to the Bank of England five years later.

Nigel's original insight remains valid today.

The next Conservative Government will keep the inflation targeting framework because the benefits of anchoring inflation expectations remain substantial.

I have said before that in office we will review, in cooperation with the independent Bank of England, what modifications are appropriate to ensure that housing costs are once again properly reflected in the target - this process is already underway at a European level but there may be a case for accelerating it.

But given the fragility and uncertainty in financial markets, let me make it absolutely clear that we have no plans to change the

CPI inflation target, and we will maintain the current arrangements and protocols for making decisions around quantitative easing.

I don't want there to be the slightest suspicion that the next Conservative Government might try to inflate its way out of the previous Government's problems.

But it is now clear to everyone that narrow inflation targeting is not in itself sufficient for macroeconomic stability.

Given what we now know about the way that unsustainable increases in debt can cause devastating financial crises, we must be as concerned about credit cycles as we have been about business cycles.

Alan Greenspan and others made the case for ignoring credit bubbles and then "mopping up" when they burst.

But even Alan now concedes that this approach has been shown to have unacceptable costs.

So as economists like Robert Shiller and others have argued, we need a more sophisticated understanding of how financial markets actually work, including the psychology that drives them away from stable equilibria.

And we need an approach that actively seeks to identify emerging imbalances and takes action to reduce them.

The question is what tools are needed to do that.

In the UK, inflation targeting succeeded in anchoring inflation expectations, but the very design of the policy framework meant that responding to an explosion in balance sheets, asset prices and macroeconomic imbalances was impossible.

Because the tools needed to deal with these imbalances had been taken away from it, the Bank of England became excessively focused on controlling consumer price inflation to the exclusion of other variables, as the Bank itself has acknowledged.

And the Financial Services Authority became a narrow financial regulator almost entirely focused on rules-based regulation.

They had neither the capacity nor the inclination to stand back and make difficult judgments about the macro context and the growth of systemic risks.

To be fair they too have also been commendably candid about those failures.

So, while much has been made of how the tripartite system led to a fatal lack of leadership when the crisis broke, the much greater failure was in the years leading up to the crisis as the imbalances built up.

Crucially, this failure was hardwired into the institutional design of the framework, and no amount of tinkering with new committees and new statutory obligations will fix it.

Indeed we are in danger of making similar mistakes in the aftermath of the crisis, with too little consideration of the impact of higher capital and liquidity requirements on overall financial conditions and the pace of recovery.

And despite everything we know about the aftermath of banking crises, there is still no single institution that is responsible for ensuring that the monetary transmission mechanism is functioning as it should, so that policy rates are properly passed through to businesses and consumers.

So we need a wholly new framework.

Some have questioned our decision to put the Bank of England in charge of macro and micro-prudential supervision.

I see it as absolutely fundamental to a new economic framework for monitoring and controlling the growth of private debt in our economy.

Only independent central banks have the broad macroeconomic understanding, the authority and the knowledge required to make the kind of macro-prudential judgments that are required now and in the future.

Of course, they must operate with a mandate from, and accountability to, the elected Government, similar to the existing inflation targeting system.

But this new role will inevitably require a degree of judgment and discretion that goes beyond the narrow rules-based system that failed either to spot or prevent the crisis.

And, because central banks are the lender of last resort, the experience of the crisis has also shown that they need to be intimately familiar with every aspect of the institutions that they may have to support.

So they must also be responsible for day-to-day micro-prudential regulation as well.

That case is particularly strong where the banking system is highly concentrated as it is in the UK, where the boundary between micro and macro-prudential regulation is not easy to define.

For example, who could deny that the micro-prudential regulation of a large international bank like Barclays, RBS or HSBC has in and of itself significant macro-prudential implications for the UK economy?

Since we've been making this argument about a new model of financial regulation, the intellectual tide has turned decisively in our favour.

The arguments we have made are the same as those that lie behind the direction of reform at the Federal Reserve and in the Bundesbank, and they are argument now publicly supported by the likes of Jacques de Larosiere, Ben Bernanke, and Stanley Fischer - the eminent monetary economist and Governor of the Central Bank of Israel.

The precise tools of macro-prudential regulation must now be the subject of intensive debate, international coordination, and ultimately experimentation.

They may include variable risk weightings for different asset classes, adjustable capital and liquidity requirements, and even more direct interventions in lending behaviour, but we should rule nothing out at this stage.

We should also recognize that no system of supervision and regulation will ever eliminate failures.

That's why we must keep up the pressure for reform so that our banking system itself is more robust to failure and the damage that failure inflicts on the broader economy is minimised.

It would be a tragedy if we ended up with a banking system that is even more concentrated, riskier and more prone to moral hazard than the one we had before the crisis.

More and better quality capital, credible resolution procedures, living wills and more competition are all important parts of the solution.

But I also believe we should pursue international agreement for a levy on the banking system, similar to the levy on wholesale funding proposed by President Obama or the levy already implemented in Sweden, as well as for structural reforms to prevent retail banks with implicit taxpayer guarantees from engaging in the riskiest activities such as large scale proprietary trading.

These would not have prevented the crisis on their own, and they cannot be a substitute for a better underlying macroeconomic and regulatory policy framework.

But together they would help to create a system that is more robust to failure.

Fiscal Policy

These are the new tools and institutions that we need to control the growth of private debt in the future.

They are a key component of moving to that new model of economic growth.

But the bigger risk to our economy now stems from an explosion in public debt.

To entrench economic stability for the long term, we need fundamental reform of our fiscal policy framework.

There is wide agreement among economists on the need for more independent scrutiny of fiscal policy to replace the discredited fiscal rules.

Conservatives first proposed that independent scrutiny more than five years ago. We have now set out in detail how that scrutiny will be performed by an Office for Budget Responsibility.

Let me say a little bit more about this Office, because I don't think people have fully appreciated what a radical departure this represents from the way Chancellors have put together Budgets in the past.

Everyone can see how the fiscal rules created in 1997 failed catastrophically.

They did nothing to prevent the Government from running a current budget deficit at the peak of the boom.

To coin a phrase, we didn't fix the roof when the sun was shining.

The flaws in the fiscal rules are now well known - they were backwards looking, so that past surpluses could be used to justify present deficits, and they were adjudicated by the Treasury with no independent oversight, undermining their credibility.

But there is also an emerging recognition in the academic literature that any system of rules is likely to be unsatisfactory - either so general as to be ineffective, or so complex as to be inflexible and impossible to enforce.

Instead there is growing support for the concept of fiscal councils that can bring independent and forward-looking scrutiny to bear on governments.

Institutions of this kind now exist in Sweden, Denmark and the Netherlands.

I believe that just as we need to move away from narrowly defined rules towards greater judgment in financial regulation, the same is true in fiscal policy.

The benefits of fiscal councils for sustainable fiscal policy could be as profound as those of independent central banks for monetary policy.

Evidence suggests that many of the same time-consistency problems that lead to inflation bias when politicians are in direct control of monetary policy can lead to deficit bias in fiscal policy.

Of course, the analogy is not exact - unelected bodies should not be given independent executive power over the levers of fiscal policy because of the fundamentally political distributive consequences of decisions over spending and tax.

But the power of a fiscal council to hold politicians to account for the fiscal implications of their tax and spending plans should not be underestimated.

These powerful arguments, and the steady erosion of public trust in official forecasts, lie behind our proposals for an independent Office for Budget Responsibility.

The OBR will be made up of a three person committee, accountable to Parliament, and a small secretariat of economists and public finance experts.

It will be responsible for publishing independent fiscal forecasts at least twice a year around the time of the Budget and PBR, based on existing government policy at the time.

And the committee will publish a recommendation for the amount of net fiscal tightening or loosening it judges necessary for the Treasury to have a better than 50% chance of achieving a forward looking mandate set by the Chancellor.

If the Chancellor chooses not to abide by that recommendation he or she will have to explain their reasoning to Parliament, but it would be a brave Chancellor who chose to do so.

At least once a year, the OBR will also publish a comprehensive assessment of the true long term sustainability of the public finances, including off balance sheet liabilities such as public sector pensions, PFI and the likely costs of an ageing population.

For the first time we will have a transparent national balance sheet.

The Office for Budget Responsibility will be up and running on a temporary basis for the first Budget of a Conservative Government, much as the Monetary Policy

Committee initially functioned for a year without underpinning legislation.

Sir Alan Budd has agreed to chair the Office for Budget Responsibility during this period. No one can doubt his independence, and I want to thank him for taking this important task on.

Whether I thank him in a couple of years' time is another matter - but that is the whole point.

So this is how we will entrench fiscal responsibility for the long term, but we also face an immediate fiscal challenge.

In the last two weeks, disagreements within the economics profession over how quickly to tackle the record budget deficit have been thrust into the spotlight.

Before I address those disagreements, it's worth remembering that there are broad areas of agreement that didn't exist even six months ago.

There is a recognition that the scale of the deficit and the rapid increase in the national debt cannot safely be ignored, and that public expenditure will have to be cut.

That is something we Conservatives have been saying since the start, and we had to face down those who said that cuts were never going to be necessary.

There is also general agreement now that Britain needs a more credible medium-term plan to deal with the deficit, as both the IMF and the OECD have argued.

The Governor of the Bank made this point yet again yesterday, as did the signatories of one of those letters to the Financial Times last week.

So when it comes to identifying the problem, the need to set out a more credible plan, and the case for having that plan independently monitored, there is broad agreement.

Where disagreements remain is on the details of the timing and pace of deficit reduction.

The economists who signed those two letters cautioning against early action are reasonable people who care deeply about the future of the British economy.

But while I respect their position, I take a different view - a view shared by the equally eminent economists who wrote to the Sunday Times, many leading business figures and crucially by international investors.

And that view is simple.

A credible plan is not really credible unless you're prepared to make a start on it this year.

Otherwise we are trying to persuade people that we will be virtuous, just not yet - and when you've been as irresponsible as Britain has been, that isn't easy.

That is my hard-headed assessment.

And it is driven by three things:

The nature of confidence; the realities of financial markets; and the practicalities of government.

Let me take each in turn.

First, confidence.

Those who recommend delay argue that when private demand is weak, cutting government spending too quickly risks undermining the recovery.

In its most simplistic form this argument fails to ask why it is that private demand is weak.

Modern economics understands the importance of expectations and confidence.

Businesses and individuals look to the future, and while they are not the perfectly rational creatures assumed by the theory of Ricardian equivalence, uncertainty over the future paths of tax rates and government spending does play an important role in their behaviour.

This is particularly true when it comes to consumer spending and business investment, and as the Governor has made clear, the Bank of

England tries to take these effects into account when making its forecasts.

So a credible fiscal consolidation plan will have a positive impact through greater certainty and confidence about the future.

Businesses can expand safer in the knowledge that an out of control budget is not going to lead to ever higher taxes.

Consumers can spend safer in the knowledge that mortgage rates will remain lower for longer.

To be fair, a more sophisticated version of the argument for delay also takes into account the complex interaction between fiscal policy and monetary conditions.

It says that at the moment, and for as long as policy and market interest rates remain low, fiscal tightening should be as gradual as possible because there is little scope for more accommodating monetary conditions to accompany it, either through lower market interest rates or through the reaction function of the Bank of England.

And only as and when monetary conditions begin to tighten can the pace of fiscal consolidation be accelerated.

But even this, more nuanced, version of the case for delay is too complacent.

For it brings me to the second consideration: the realities of financial markets.

Experience shows that market adjustments tend to be neither smooth nor gradual - instead reassessments are more likely to be sudden and brutal.

The luxury of waiting for monetary conditions to tighten before embarking on fiscal tightening may not be one that we are afforded.

That is why the experiences of other countries right now, not just Greece but also Ireland, Spain, Portugal, Poland and others, as well as examples like Sweden and Canada in the past, are so important.

If markets start to lose confidence in a country and interest rates are driven up, recovery is undermined and the inevitable cuts to spending end up being deeper and more savage than would have been necessary to maintain market confidence in the first place.

Take a look at the measures the government was forced to implement across the Irish sea.

That is not a risk that I am prepared to take.

Already the yield spread between 10 year gilts and 10 year German bonds is more than 90 basis points, compared to 70 basis points for Spain and 110 basis points for Portugal.

In the most extreme cases, countries that lose the confidence of markets effectively lose their sovereignty.

As Goran Persson, the Social Democrat Prime Minister of Sweden who eliminated a huge budget deficit following a financial crisis and a deep recession in the early 1990s, used to say, "a country in debt is not free".

This is why credibility is so vital.

Far from accepting "as binding the views of the same financial markets whose mistakes precipitated the crisis in the first place", as one of last week's letters to the FT put it, establishing credibility does exactly the reverse - it buys you more freedom from the very real constraints of financial markets.

How much better to make difficult decisions about spending on your own terms and at your own speed than to have them forced upon you on somebody else's terms?

So undermining credibility by giving the impression that cuts can be avoided, or by suggesting that unexpected improvements in the public finances will lead to more spending, only makes deeper cuts more likely.

But the decisive case for making an early start on reducing our record deficit is not only based on confidence and the need to establish credibility.

It also draws on an understanding of the realities of government - in particular institutional inertia and the difficulty of real reform.

These considerations don't appear in most economists' models.

Economists usually talk about fiscal tightening in billions of pounds or percentages of GDP, but cutting spending is not simply a matter of numbers in a Budget Red Book.

It is a myth, perpetrated by politicians, that all Ministers have to do is sit in their Whitehall offices pulling levers, and things change on the ground.

More often than not, the levers aren't connected to anything.

Real change that drives up productivity is a difficult process.

If unstable financial markets do force emergency cuts, then those are precisely the conditions in which their impact on the poorest in society and the quality of public services is likely to be greatest.

As Gordon Brown told his party conference when he was Shadow Chancellor: "Losing control of public spending doesn't help the poor."

Making an early start, on your own terms, creates the space for better targeted cuts.

It will give more time for public sector reforms to take effect so that lower spending is delivered through greater efficiency not cuts to the front line.

And it makes it easier to preserve public support for difficult decisions by protecting the poorest and most vulnerable.

A key lesson from the successful examples from around the world of fiscal consolidation is that you must be able to demonstrate that 'we are all in this together' in order to maintain a coalition for action.

So that is why we will make an early start - in order to bring confidence to the economy, establish the credibility with markets that buys you time,

and to ensure that spending cuts are well targeted.

Let me explain how a new government will do that.

There will be three clear phases to our plan of action.

Phase One involves finding out the truth.

Within days of taking office we will establish our new independent Office for Budget Responsibility.

We have put in place the plans and the people to be ready to do that on a non-statutory basis, until the legislation is in place to make it permanent.

The Office will help us publish a truly independent audit of the public finances before the first Budget.

So everyone will know the true state of the nation's balance sheet.

And everyone will be able to see independent forecasts for growth.

Only then will anyone know the true scale of the fiscal challenge that faces whoever forms the next government.

Phase Two is the Budget.

This will take place within 50 days.

It will set out the overall fiscal path and spending totals that we will stick to over the years ahead.

As I have made clear, our aim will be to eliminate the bulk of the structural current budget deficit over a Parliament.

That is what the Governor of the Bank of England has called for and I agree with him.

The Budget will set out some of the cross-cutting measures on pay, the cost of Whitehall, the review of the pension age, and the largest public sector pensions, that will help to put our public finances on a sustainable footing.

Crucially, the first Budget will also contain measures to boost enterprise, encourage new jobs and show that Britain is open for business.

We will take targeted steps to reduce some budgets in-year - and we have set out some specific examples - in order to build credibility and make a start on reducing the deficit.

The scale of these steps will be informed by that proper audit of the nation's finances, that independent assessment of growth and discussions with the independent Bank of England about the scope for monetary policy to remain supportive.

At the same time the rest of government will be embarking on the major structural reforms to the public services that will, over time, deliver the lasting productivity gains that drive real value for money.

Phase Three is the Spending Review

Over the Summer we will work flat out to conduct the detailed departmental Spending Review for the years after 2011 that the current government has simply refused to carry out, and publish that results of that review in the Autumn.

The only possible reason why the Treasury has not already produced a Spending Review is that the Government do not want to spell out the difficult decisions that even their own spending plans imply.

We will not hesitate to take the difficult decisions to get Britain working.

'A New Economic Model'
So this is the new economic framework for monetary and fiscal policy that we need to ensure that private and public debt are sustainable in the future.

But given that we cannot go back to the last decade's debt-fuelled model of growth, the question I am asked most often at the moment, is "where is the growth going to come from?"

The answer is the final part of this new economic model.

The economics profession is in broad agreement that the recovery will only be sustainable if it is accompanied by an internal and external rebalancing of our economy: in other words a higher savings rate, more business investment, and rising net exports.

Economic theory and evidence both suggest that the macroeconomic policy combination most likely to encourage that adjustment is tight fiscal policy, supportive monetary policy and countercyclical financial regulation.

But that on its own will not be enough.

We need a program of supply side reform that is no less urgent or radical than the reforms of the 1980s and 1990s.

When our households, our banks and our government are so indebted, raising the real rate of return on investment is the only sustainable route to prosperity.

All the evidence suggests that Britain's trend rate of growth has declined over the last decade.

And as we saw in the 1980s and 1990s, supply side reforms can take some years before their full effect is felt.

But a new government presents a golden opportunity to set out a new direction and harvest some of the long-term benefits up front.

By embarking upon a series of reforms that will raise the real return on investment, we can raise the rate of investment right now.

That's why I have pledged that a Conservative Government will use the opportunity of a change of government to send the signal that Britain is once again open for business.

And in order to bring some accountability to economic policy, I have set out eight benchmarks for the next Parliament against which you will be able to judge whether a Conservative Government is delivering on this new economic model.

So we will maintain Britain's AAA credit rating.

We will increase saving, business investment and exports as a share of GDP.

The plans I announced at the weekend to sell in due course the government's stakes in RBS and Lloyds will help to encourage millions of people to start saving and investing for the future, often for the first time.

We will improve Britain's international rankings for tax competitiveness and business regulation with specific measures on corporation tax and regulatory budgets.

We will reduce youth unemployment and reduce the number of children in workless households as part of our strategy for tackling poverty and inequality.

We will raise the private sector's share of the economy in all regions of the country, especially outside London and the South East.

And we will reduce UK greenhouse gas emissions and increase our share of global markets for low carbon technologies.

But perhaps the greatest challenge is reforming the public sector itself.

The part of our economy that is responsible for delivering this framework for economic success is the one that has performed the worst of any sector over the last decade.

Public sector productivity has actually fallen since 1997.

Indeed, if productivity in the public sector had grown at the same rate as in private sector services, we could now have the same quality of public services for £60 billion less each year.

A radical program of public sector reform is not just a fiscal necessity, it is vital if we are to deliver the world class education and welfare services that support a competitive economy.

So we will raise productivity growth in the public sector by increasing diversity of provision, extending payment by results, giving more power to consumers and improving financial controls.

We will expect productivity improvements to match the best of the private sector.

And crucially, the Treasury will return to its core role of ensuring value for money for the only interest group it should represent - taxpayers.

There will be no more empire building or attempts to interfere in every area of government policy.

How can I put it in a topical way?

You will have a Chancellor and a Prime Minister united with the common goal of unleashing the forces of enterprise.

Conclusion
Delivering the new economic model that I have set out today will not be easy.

Britain cannot run away from its problems. And if we fail to learn the lessons of the last decade, we are doomed to repeat them.

We have to deal with our debts to get our economy back on its feet.

The core values that we need to apply are responsibility and accountability.

Over the five years that I have been in this job I have put fiscal and financial responsibility at the heart of my approach.

I resisted the calls to offer up front unfunded tax cuts. I said that an economy built on debt was living on borrowed time - and so it was.

I have also been straight with the British people about the challenges ahead.

I said that whoever won the election would have to cut spending.

And I have set out the benchmarks against which we can be held accountable.

Our ambition is nothing less than a new economic model for Britain.

Let us move from an economy built on debt to an economy that saves and invests for the future.

Appendix II

Thomas Hodgskin's Early Business Cycle Theory
– based on Government encouraged Credit Expansion

Hodgskin's ideas on the nature of business cycles were thinly scattered through his writings. An early example can be found in a letter published on 12th Feb. 1826 in the *Trades' Newspaper - Effects of Repealing the Corn Laws*. These early conjectures were conceived around the idea that capitalists, being over-stimulated by government actions and encouragements, periodically overtraded or inappropriately invested. This over-stimulation resulted from non-economic or political circumstances; i.e. it was exogenous in character.

This can be seen in Hodgskin's letter which defended bankers but laid the blame with the government for the depression that followed the short-lived boom of late 1825.

> A more efficient and certain cause can be found in ... the speculation of the capitalist and the master

> manufacturer, which were founded in the hopes of advantages that have never been realised ... I attribute [this] ... to the speeches and writings of the ministerial part of the Government, ... they have flattered the cupidite and stimulated the enterprise of our manufacturers and merchants, by talking of the increased market they were to find for their commodities. The latter eagerly hastened to supply the imaginary market. ... These speculations turned out not profitable – they became bankrupt, and distress among the workmen ... has been the consequence. (Hodgskin, *TN.*, 12th Feb. 1826)

In *Natural and Artificial Right of Property Contrasted* the subject of business cycles was broached again with reference to the legal right of property and the businessmen's unreliable expectations.

> When we look at the commercial history of our country, and see the false hopes of our merchants and manufacturers leading to periodical commercial convulsions, we are compelled to conclude, that they have not the same source as the regular and harmonious external

world. ... Starts of national prosperity, followed by bankruptcy and ruin, have the same source then as fraud and forgery. To our legal right of property, we are indebted for those gleams of false wealth and real panic, which, within the last fifty years, have so frequently shook, to its centre, the whole trading world. (Hodgskin, 1832, p.155-6)

Hodgskin's interest does not appear resurrected again until his review of McCulloch's *Treatise on the Circumstances which Determine the Rate of Wages* that showed that he conceived that the cyclical booms could involve an increase in consumption without an appropriate increase in capital:

It has always been the argument, of the Economist, that in those years [1842-46] capital was much misapplied and wasted; and hence the revulsion of 1847-8. There was something else, therefore, besides the quantity of capital which determined the employment and the wages of labour between 1842 and 1846, and that something every person knows, was a delusive and *false hope* in capitalists, or those

> who could obtain credit, which gave a wonderful extension to employment without any corresponding increase in capital. The quantity of capital was the ultimate test, indeed, of the validity of credit; it proved the credit to have been fallacious – the hopes to have been a delusion; but in the meantime, the people were employed, the wages paid and consumed; (Hodgskin, *E.*, 27th Dec. 1851, p.1440)

The *Economist*'s position was generally that the "delusive and *false hope* in capitalists" stemmed from the government's exaggerated assertions and exogenous support regarding the expansion of railways, as such this interference had economically negative consequences.

Whilst it would be unrealistic to assert that Hodgskin possessed anything like a fully worked out theory of business cycles, the above passages illustrate that he was well aware of the problem. However, rather than lay the blame on changes to population or simple bad luck, he sought an economic answer primarily with government actions as the root cause of the difficulties.

To Hodgskin's mind, the problems associated with business cycles were caused by factors outside the "regular and harmonious" conditions of an unfettered market, which would otherwise have progressed or grown in a manner favourable to mankind's economic needs. As such these outside influences were exogenous to the economic ideal of a pure market economy.

Bibliography

Adaman, F. & Madra, Y. M. (2002): *Theorizing the "Third Sphere": A Critique of the Persistence of the "Economistic Fallacy".* In the *Journal of Economic Issues*, Vol. 36, No. 4, p.1045-1078.

Alesina, A. (2010, April): *Fiscal Adjustments: Lessons from Recent History.* ECOFIN Meeting, Madrid.

Alesina, A. & Ardagna, S. (2010): *Large Changes in Fiscal Policy: Taxes versus Spending.* In *Tax Policy and the Economy*, Vol. 24, 35-68.

Allen, K. (2014, March 7): *£20bn black hole in public finances would mean more austerity or tax rises.* Retrieved April 18, 2014, from The Guardian:
www.theguardian.com/business/2014/mar/07/black- hole-public-finances-austerity-ft-obr

Allen, K. (2014, March 10): *UK GDP to exceed pre-recession peak this summer, business body predicts.* Retrieved April 18, 2014, from The Guardian:
www.theguardian.com/business/2014/mar/10/uk-gdp-pre-recession-peak-predicts

Allen, K. (2014, March 19): *Budget 2014: economy predicted to return to pre-crisis level this year.* Retrieved April 19, 2014, from The Guardian:
www.theguardian.com/uk-news/2014/mar/19/budget-2014-economy-predicted-pre-crisis-level

Armitstead, L. (2013, February 24): *Chancellor Must 'Ease Pace' of Austerity in Wake of UK Credit Rating Downgrade.* Retrieved January 24, 2014, from The Telegraph:
http://www.telegraph.co.uk/finance/economics/9891209/Chancellor-must-ease-pace-of-austerity-in-wake-of-UK-credit-rating-downgrade.html

Bagaria, N., Holland, D., Portes, J. & Reenen, J. V. (2012, August 14): *The impact of alternative paths of fiscal consolidation on output and employment in the UK.* Retrieved January 31, 2014, from VoxEU:
http://www.voxeu.org/article/alternatives-austerity-effect-jobs-and-incomes-uk

Bălan, Sergiu (2012): *Substantivism, Culturalism and Formalism in Economic Anthropology.* Retrieved April 15, 2014, from:
http://cogito.ucdc.ro/en/2012/vol4n2/en/4_substantivism-culturalism-and-formalism-in-economic-anthropology.pdf

Balls, E. (2014, 14th April): *Why Labour won't stop talking about the cost of living crisis.* Retrieved April 16, 2014, from The Guardian:
www.theguardian.com/commentisfree/2014/apr/14/labour-party-cost-of-living-crisis

Balls, E. (April 2014): *'There is an alternative' – Ed Balls' speech at Bloomberg.* Retrieved April 19, 2014, from:
www.edballs.co.uk/blog/?p=907

Ball, L. M., Furceri, D., Leigh, M. D. & Loungani, M. P. (2013): *The Distributional Effects of Fiscal Consolidation* (No. 13-151). International Monetary Fund.

Bank of England. (2013, October): *Trends in Lending.* Bank of England. (2013). *Quarterly Bulletin 2013 Q1. Volume 53 No. 1*

Bank of England. (2013): *News Release - The Outlook for the UK Economy - Speech by Paul Fisher.* Retrieved April 19, 2014, from Bank of England:
www.bankofengland.co.uk/publications/Pages/news/2013/067.aspx

Barker, A., Schäfer , D. & Parker, G. (2013, September 25): *George Osborne takes EU to court over bank bonus cap.* Retrieved March 11, 2014, from:
http://www.ft.com/cms/s/0/0f54735a-25f6-11e3-8ef6-00144feab7de.html?siteedition=uk#axzz2vgIq6Hmv

BBC News. (2008, September 29): *B&B nationalisation is confirmed.* Retrieved April 19, 2014, from BBC News:
news.bbc.co.uk/1/hi/business/7641193.stm

BBC News. (2009, December 30): *Gordon Brown's new year message looks to election.* Retrieved April 19, 2014, from BBC News:
news.bbc.co.uk/1/hi/uk_politics/8434137.stm

BBC News. (2010, January 9): *Alistair Darling warns of tough spending cuts.* Retrieved April 19, 2014, from BBC News:
news.bbc.co.uk/1/hi/8449716.stm

BBC News. (2010, September 20): *Moody's Hails UK Austerity Effort*. Retrieved January 24, 2014, from BBC News:
http://www.bbc.co.uk/news/business-11373977

BBC News. (2012, September 28): *France budget: Taxes favoured over spending cuts*. Retrieved April 17, 2014, from BBC News:
www.bbc.co.uk/news/world-europe-19754016

BBC News. (2013, September 27): *David Cameron: Hard decisions on economy 'paying off'*. Retrieved April 17, 2014, from BBC News:
www.bbc.co.uk/news/uk-politics-24301391

BBC News. (2013, April 19): *Fitch downgrades UK credit rating to AA+*. Retrieved March 11, 2014, from:
www.bbc.co.uk/news/business-22219382

BBC News. (2013, December 29): *France's 75% tax rate gains approval by top court*. Retrieved April 17, 2014, from BBC News:
www.bbc.co.uk/news/business-25541739

BBC News. (2013, September 10): *Q&A: What is the Tobin Tax on financial trading?* Retrieved April 28, 2014, from BBC News:
www.bbc.co.uk/news/business-15552412

BBC News. (2014, January 28): *UK economy growing at fastest rate since 2007*. Retrieved April 18, 2014, from BBC News:
www.bbc.co.uk/news/business-25926648

BBC News. (2014, April 16): *UK unemployment falls to five-year low of 2.2m.* Retrieved April 17, 2014, from BBC News: www.bbc.co.uk/news/business-27046681

BBC News. (2014, March 7): *Lawyers stage second walkout over legal aid cuts.* Retrieved March 11, 2014, from: www.bbc.co.uk/news/uk-26472809

BBC News. (2014, February 19): *UK unemployment falls by 125,000 to 2.34 million.* Retrieved March 11, 2014, from: www.bbc.co.uk/news/business-26255696

BBC News. (2014, January 22): *George Osborne: 'Good news on borrowing and jobs'.* Retrieved February 17, 2014, from BBC News:
http://www.bbc.co.uk/news/business-25849238

BBC News. (2018, December 18th): *Student loan ruling adds £12bn to government borrowing.* Retrieved March 20, 2019, from BBC News:
https://www.bbc.co.uk/news/education-46591500

Bell, D.N.F. & Blanchflower, D. (2013, May): *Underemployment in the UK Revisited. National Institute Economic Review 224*, 8-22.

Besley, T. & Hennessy, P. (2009, July 22): *Letter from British Academy to Her Majesty the Queen.*

Blanchard, O. (1990): *Can Severe Fiscal Contractions Be Expansionary? Tales of Two Small European Countries: Comment.* NBER Macroeconomics Annual, Vol. 5, 111-116.

Blanchard, O., Dell'Ariccia, G. & Mauro, P. (2010): *Rethinking Macroeconomic Policy.* Journal of Money, Credit and Banking, 42(s1), 199-215.

Blanchard, O. & Leigh, D. (2013): *Growth Forecast Errors and Fiscal Multipliers.* IMF Working Papers.

Blyth, M. (2013): *Austerity: The History of a Dangerous Idea.* New York City: Oxford University Press.

Blyth, M. (2013, June): *Austerity – The History of a Dangerous Idea.* Retrieved April 16, 2014, from YouTube: https://www.youtube.com/watch?v=JQuHSQXxsjM

Blyth, M. (2013, November 13): *Eternal austerity makes complete sense – if you're rich.* Retrieved April 21, 2014, from The Guardian: www.theguardian.com/commentisfree/2013/nov/15/eternal-austerity-makes-sense-if-rich-david-cameron

Bowers, S. (2013, March 19): *Icelandic bank Kaupthing's top executives indicted over market rigging.* Retrieved April 17, 2014, from The Guardian: www.theguardian.com/business/2013/mar/19/kaupthing-executives-indicted-for-market-rigging

Boyer, R. (2012): *The Four Fallacies of Contemporary Austerity Policies: The Lost Keynesian Legacy.* Cambridge Journal of Economics, Vol. 36, 283-312.

Buchanan, J.M. & Wagner, R.E. (1977): *Democracy in Deficit: The Political Legacy of Lord Keynes.*

Cabinet Office. (2010, May 18): *Building the Big Society.* Retrieved April 17, 2014, from: https://www.gov.uk/government/publications/building-the-big-society

Cable, V. (2013, March 6): *When the facts change, should I change my mind?* Retrieved April 16, 2014, from New Statesman: http://www.newstatesman.com/politics/politics/2013/03/when-facts-change-should-i-change-my-mind

Cameron, S. (2014, April 17): *Why should the innocent pay for justice?* Retrieved April 18, 2014, from The Telegraph: www.telegraph.co.uk/news/uknews/law-and-order/10770324/Why-should-the-innocent-pay-for-justice.html

Chakraborrty, A. (2013, November 4): *Rail privatisation: legalised larceny.* Retrieved March 30, 2014, from The Guardian: www.theguardian.com/commentisfree/2013/nov/04/rail-privatisation-train-operators-profit

Chartered Institute of Personnel and Development. (2013, August 5): *Zero hours contracts more widespread than thought - but only minority of zero hours workers want to work more hours.* Retrieved April 25, 2014, from CIPD: www.cipd.co.uk/pressoffice/press-releases/zero-hours-contracts-more-widespread-thought-050813.aspx

Chote, R. (2013, March 8): Retrieved January 31, 2014, from Office for Budget Responsibility: http://budgetresponsibility.org.uk/wordpress/docs/Letter-from-Robert-Chote-to-Prime-Minister.pdf

Chowdhury, A. & Islam, I. (2012, February 28): *Revisiting the evidence on expansionary fiscal austerity: Alesina's hour?* Retrieved November 27, 2013, from VoxEU: http://www.voxeu.org/debates/commentaries/revisiting-evidence-expansionary-fiscal-austerity-alesina-s-hour

Clark, T. (2014, April 25). *Dead roots lurk beneath the green shoots of Britain's economic recovery.* Retrieved April 25, 2014, from The Guardian: www.theguardian.com/books/2014/apr/25/dead-roots-beneath-green-shoots-britains-economic-recovery-austerity-recession

Conservative Party. (2010): *The Conservative Manifesto 2010: Invitation to Join the Government of Britain*

Conway, E. (2013, April 16): *IMF Inflicts 'Double Blow' On George Osborne.* Retrieved March 4, 2014, from Sky News: http://news.sky.com/story/1078887/imf-inflicts-double-blow-on-george-osborne

Crawford, R., Emmerson, C., & Keynes, S. (2013, April): *Deficit Unchanged.* Retrieved January 28, 2014, from Institute for Fiscal Studies:
http://www.ifs.org.uk/publications/6663

Crotty, J. (2012): *The Great Austerity War: What Caused the US Deficit Crisis and Who Should Pay to Fix It? Cambridge Journal of Economics*, Vol. 36, 79-104.

Crouch, C. (2011). *The Strange Non-Death of Neo-Liberalism.* Polity.

Day, F.G. (ed.): *The Definitive Labour Defended. Collected Works of Thomas Hodgskin, Vol. 1.* Praescientia Press, Wroclaw, Poland.

Delamothe, T. & Godlee, F. (2011): *Dr Lansley's Monster. BMJ, 342,* d408.

DeLong, J.B. (2012, September 23): *Confidence Fairies and Inflation-Expectation Imps.* Retrieved April 19, 2014, from:
delong.typepad.com/sdj/2012/09/confidence-fairies-and-inflation-expectation-imps-paul-krugman-smacks-down-robert-waldmanns-and-brad-delong.html

Department for Transport & Office of Rail Regulation. (2011): *Realising the Potential of GB Rail: Report of the Rail Value for Money Study – Summary Report*. Retrieved March 29, 2014, from:
https://www.gov.uk/government/uploads/system/uploads/attachment_data/file/4203/realising-the-potential-of-gb-rail-summary.pdf

Dias, D. (2014, January 6): *Why barristers walked out of court*. Retrieved March 11, 2014, from:
http://blogs.lse.ac.uk/politicsandpolicy/archives/38794

Drayton, Richard (2013): Letter: *"The Shit We're In"*. London Review of Books vol.35. No. 2 – 25th January 2013:
https://www.lrb.co.uk/v35/n02/letters

Eaton, George (2013): *Cameron is wrong: the spending cuts are ideological*. The New Statesmen, 31st December 2010:
https://www.newstatesman.com/blogs/the-staggers/2010/12/spending-cuts-tax-ideological

Economist, The. (2010, July 1): *Austerity Alarm*. Retrieved April 20, 2014, from The Economist:
www.economist.com/node/16485318?story_id=16485318

Electoral Commission. (2018): *Referendum on the UK's membership of the European Union.* [Online] Available at: https://www.electoralcommission.org.uk/find-information-by-subject/elections-and-referendums/past-elections-and-referendums/eu-referendum

Elliott, L. (2013, April 18): *George Osborne told by IMF chief: rethink your austerity plan.* Retrieved March 4, 2014, from The Guardian: http://www.theguardian.com/politics/2013/apr/18/george-osborne-imf-austerity

Elliott, L. (2013, May 23): *Falling investment poses another problem for Osborne.* Retrieved April 20, 2014, from The Guardian: www.theguardian.com/business/economics-blog/2013/may/23/uk-business-investment

Elliott, L. (2013, May 26): *Britain is a lab rat for George Osborne's austerity programme experiment.* Retrieved April 16, 2014, from The Guardian: www.theguardian.com/business/2013/may/26/britain-osborne-austerity-programme-experiment

Elliott, L. (2014, January 27): *Vince Cable attacks 'ideological' cuts and says UK's recovery is wrong kind.* Retrieved March 11, 2014, from: www.theguardian.com/politics/2014/jan/27/vince-cable-attacks-ideological-cuts-uk-recovery

Elliott, L. (2014, April 7): *Rising UK population undermines good news on GDP recovery, ONS says.* Retrieved April 18, 2014, from The Guardian: www.theguardian.com/uk-news/2014/apr/07/ /rising-uk-population-gdp-recovery-ons

Elliott, L. & Monaghan, A. (2014, February 12): *Interest rates on hold as Bank says recovery 'unsustainable'.* Retrieved April 19, 2014, from The Guardian: www.theguardian.com/business/2014/feb/12/inter est-rates-economic-recovery-unsustainable

Ford, R. & Goodwin, M. (2014): *Revolt on the right: Explaining support for the radical right in Britain.* 1st ed. Oxfordshire: Routledge Publishers

Fraser, N. (2011): *Marketization, Social Protection, Emancipation: Toward a Neo-Polanyian Conception of Capitalist Crisis. Business as Usual: The Roots of the Global Financial Crisis*, 137-157.

Freud, D. (2013, July 2): *Lords Hansard: Column 1071.* Retrieved April 28, 2014, from: www.publications.parliament.uk/pa/ld201314/ldha nsrd/text/130702-0001.htm

Goodwin, M. & Heath, O. (2016): *Brexit and the left behind: a tale of two countries.* [Online] Available at: http://eprints.lse.ac.uk/73016/1/blogs.lse.ac.uk-Brexit%20and%20the%20left%20behind%20a%20tale%20of%20two%20countries.pdf [Accessed 19 2 2018].

Giavazzi, F., & Pagano, M. (1990): Can Severe Fiscal Contractions Be Expansionary? Tales of Two Small European Countries. *NBER Macroeconomics Annual*, Vol. 5, 75-111.

Gray, J. (2009). *Gray's Anatomy:* London: Allen Lane.

Gray, J. (2010, January 7): *The Neoliberal State.* Retrieved April 21, 2014, from New Statesman: www.newstatesman.com/non-fiction/2010/01/neoliberal-state-market-social

Gray, J. (2013, May 9): *The Real Karl Marx.* Retrieved April 20, 2014, from The New York Review of Books: www.nybooks.com/articles/archives/2013/may/09/real-karl-marx/

Green, S & Blyth, M. (2013, April 11): *Austerity's Big Bait-and-Switch.* Retrieved March 11, 2014, from: http://blogs.hbr.org/2013/04/austerirys-big-bait-and-switch/

Grimshaw, D. & Rubery, J. (2012): *The end of the UK's liberal collectivist social model? The implications of the coalition government's policy during the austerity crisis.* Cambridge Journal of Economics, Vol. *36*, 105-126.

Harvey, D. (2005): *A Brief History of Neoliberalism.* New York: Oxford University Press.

Harvey, D. (2007): *Neoliberalism as Creative Destruction. The ANNALS of the American Academy of Political and Social Science 2007*; 610; 21-44.

Hodgskin, Thomas (1867): *Theory of Capital.* Brighton Guardian – 2nd January 1867.

Hopkin, J. (2017): *When Polanyi Met Farage: Market fundamentalism, economic nationalism and Britain's Exit from the European Union. British Journal of Politics and International Relations,* 19(3), pp. 465-478.

Hutton, W. (2010, June 20): *There is no logic to the brutish cuts that George Osborne is proposing.* Retrieved March 11, 2014, from:
http://www.theguardian.com/commentisfree/2010/jun/20/budget-cuts-george-osborne

Inglehart, R. & Norris, P. (2016): *Trump, Brexit and the rise of populism.* [Online] Available at:
https://research.hks.harvard.edu/publications/getFile.aspx?Id=1401 [Accessed 23 3 2018].

Inman, P. (2009, August 27): *Financial Services Authority chairman backs tax on 'socially useless' banks.* Retrieved April 19, 2014, from The Guardian:
www.theguardian.com/business/2009/aug/27/fsa-bonus-city-banks-tax

Inman, P. (2010, November 4): *George Osborne accused of misleading public over UK bankruptcy claim.* Retrieved April 17, 2014, from The Guardian: www.theguardian.com/politics/2010/nov/04/george-osborne-misleading-crisis-claims

Inman, P. (2011, March 1): *Bank of England governor blames spending cuts on bank bailouts.* Retrieved April 17, 2014, from The Guardian: www.theguardian.com/business/2011/mar/01/mervyn-king-blames-banks-cuts

Inman, P. (2013, June 27): *IFS analysis of spending review highlights tax shortfall.* Retrieved April 18, 2014, from The Guardian: www.theguardian.com/politics/2013/jun/27/spending-review-ifs-analysis

International Monetary Fund. (2010, October): *World Economic Outlook: Recovery, Risk, and Rebalancing.*

Jakab, Zoltan, and Kumhof, Michael (2015): *Banks are not intermediaries of loanable funds - and why this matters.* Bank of England Working Paper No. 529.

Jakab, Zoltan, and Kumhof, Michael (2019): *Banks are not intermediaries of loanable funds – facts, theory and evidence.* Bank of England Working Paper No. 761.

Jayadev, A. & Konczal, M. (2010): *The Boom Not the Slump: The Right Time for Austerity.* The Roosevelt Institute.

Johnson, S. & Kwak, J. (2011): *13 Bankers: The Wall Street Takeover and the Next Financial Meltdown.* Vintage Books.

Jordà, O. & Taylor, A.M. (2013): *The Time for Austerity: Estimating the Average Treatment Effect of Fiscal Policy.* Federal Reserve Bank of San Francisco Working Paper 2013-25

Kates, S. (2012): Alesina and the Keynesians: Austerity and Say's Law. *Atlantic Economic Journal*, Vol. 40, 401-415.

Keohane, D. (2013, May 31): *A UK deleveraging disagreement.* Retrieved April 19, 2014, from FT Alphaville: ftalphaville.ft.com/2013/05/31/1521412/a-uk-deleveraging-disagreement/

King, L., Kitson, M., Konzelmann, S., & Wilkinson, F. (2012): Making the Same Mistake Again - Or is This Time Different? *Cambridge Journal of Economics*, Vol. 36, 1-15.

Kingsley, P. (2012, August 7): *Financial Crisis: Timeline.* Retrieved April 19, 2014, from The Guardian: www.theguardian.com/business/2012/aug/07/credit-crunch-boom-bust-timeline

Klein, N. (2007): *The Shock Doctrine: The Rise of Disaster Capitalism.* London: Penguin.

Koo, R. (2011, December): *The World in Balance Sheet Recession: Causes, Cure, and Politics*. Real World Economics Review 58, 19-37.

Krugman, P. (2012, September 23): *Expectations and the Confidence Fairy*. Retrieved April 19, 2014, from New York Times: http://krugman.blogs.nytimes.com/2012/09/23/expectations-and-the-confidence-fairy/

Laws, David (2012): The Orange Book: *Eight Years On. Economic Affairs*, Volume 32, Issue 2, 31-35.

Lawson, T. (2006): The Nature of Heterodox Economics. *Cambridge Journal of Economics*, Vol. 30, Issue 4, 483-505.

Linton, D. (2014, February 5): *Revealed, Soaring Cost to You of the Government Cuts.* Manchester Evening News.

London Review of Books. (2013, January 24): *Letters: The Shit We're In.* Retrieved April 28, 2014, from London Review of Books: www.lrb.co.uk/v35/n02/letters#letter1

McCulloch, John Ramsey (1851): *Treatise on the Circumstances which Determine the Rate of Wages and the Condition of the Labouring Classes.* Longman, Brown, Green, and Longmans, London.

Mason, R. (2013, December 1): *Labour would seek budget surplus in next parliament, says Ed Balls.* Retrieved April 18, 2014, from The Guardian: www.theguardian.com/politics/2013/dec/01/labour-seeks-budget-surplus-ed-balls

Mill, J.S. (1844): *On the Words Productive and Unproductive.* From the Collected Works of J.S. Mill, Vol. 4 (1967), University of Toronto Press

Milne, S. (2013, February 26): *George Osborne hasn't just failed – this is an economic disaster.* Retrieved April 17, 2014, from The Guardian: www.theguardian.com/commentisfree/2013/feb/26/george-osborne-has-not-just-failed

Milne, S. (2013, August 6): *Zero-hours contracts: in Cameron's Britain, the dockers' line-up is back.* Retrieved April 25, 2014, from The Guardian: www.theguardian.com/commentisfree/2013/aug/06/david-cameron-britain-dockers-line-up-back

Molloy, C. (2014, January 9): *'No hospital will be safe' from Clause 118.* Retrieved March 11, 2014, from: www.opendemocracy.net/ournhs/caroline-molloy/no-hospital-will-be-safe-from-clause-118

Monaghan, A. (2014, March 18): *UK austerity measures likely to hurt society's poorest, OECD warns.* Retrieved April 18, 2014, from The Guardian: www.theguardian.com/uk-news/2014/mar/18/poverty-benefits-cuts-uk-oecd

Monaghan, A. (2014, February 7): *Real wages likely to take six years to return to pre-crisis level.* Retrieved April 18, 2014, from The Guardian: www.theguardian.com/money/2014/feb/07/wages-six-years-pre-crisis

Moya, E. (2010, June 22): *Budget 2010: Britain likely to keep AAA credit rating.* Retrieved January 28, 2014, from The Guardian: http://www.theguardian.com/business/2010/jun/22/britain-aaa-credit-rating

National Audit Office. (2010, December 15): *Maintaining the Financial Stability of UK Banks: Update on the Support Schemes.*

National Audit Office. (2010, December 15): *Maintaining the Financial Stability of UK Banks: Update on the Support Schemes.*

New Economics Foundation. (2014): *Economic Healthcheck: A Return to Growth, But No Recovery.*

OECD. (2012): "Fiscal Consolidation: *How Much is Needed to Reduce Debt to a Prudent Level?", OECD Economics Department Policy Notes,* No. 11, April.

Office for Budget Responsibility. (2010, June): *Budget Forecast.*

Office for Budget Responsibility. (2012, December): *Economic and Fiscal Outlook.*

Office for Budget Responsibility. (2013, October): *Forecast Evaluation Report.*

Office for Budget Responsibility. (2013, December). *Economic and Fiscal Outlook.*

Office for Budget Responsibility. (2014, March): *Economic and Fiscal Outlook.*

Office for National Statistics. (2013, December 13): *Business Investment, Q3 2013 Revised Results.*

Office for National Statistics. (2014, February 26): *Statistical Bulletin: Second Estimate of GDP, Q4 2013.*

Office for National Statistics. (2014, April 7): *Measuring National Well-Being: Economic Well-Being.* Retrieved April 25, 2014, from ONS: http://www.ons.gov.uk/ons/dcp171766_358832.pdf

Osborne, G. (2010, February 24): *George Osborne: Mais Lecture - A New Economic Model.* Retrieved February 4, 2014, from Total Politics: http://www.totalpolitics.com/speeches/economics/economic-policy/35193/george-osborne-mais-lecture-a-new-economic-model.thtml

Osborne, G. (2010, June 22): *Budget 2010: Full text of George Osborne's statement*. Retrieved April 15, 2014, from The Telegraph: http://www.telegraph.co.uk/finance/budget/7846849/Budget-2010-Full-text-of-George-Osbornes-statement.html

Pfeffer, C. (2014): *Rethinking resistance in development studies. Journal for the German Development Institute,* 30(1), pp. 67-69.

Polanyi, K. (1944): *The Great Transformation: The Political and Economic Origins of Our Time.* Beacon Press edition (2001); Boston, Massachusetts.

Polanyi, K. (1977). *The Livelihood of Man.* London: Academic Press.

Portes, J. (2013, March 21): *'We've Cut the Deficit by a Third' - True - Here's What the Chancellor Didn't Say.* Retrieved January 31, 2014, from The Huffington Post: http://www.huffingtonpost.co.uk/jonathan-portes/budget-2013-what-george-osborne-didnt-say_b_2926842.html

Portes, J. (2013, April 9): *Recessions and recoveries: a historical perspective (updated April 9, 2013).* Retrieved from NIESR: www.niesr.ac.uk/blog/recessions-and-recoveries-historical-perspective-updated-april-9-2013#.U09nlfldWSo

Portes, J. (2013, September 10): *What Osborne won't admit: growth has increased because of slower cuts.* Retrieved March 4, 2014, from New Statesman: http://www.newstatesman.com/politics/2013/09/what-osborne-wont-admit-growth-has-increased-because-slower-cuts

Portes, J. (2013, October 10): *Fiscal Consolidation and Growth: What's Going On?* Retrieved April 25, 2014, from NIESR: http://niesr.ac.uk/blog/fiscal-consolidation-and-growth-whats-going#.U1muP_ldWSp

Public Interest Lawyers. (2013): Supreme Court Dismisses the Government's Appeal on the "Back to Work" Regulations. Retrieved March 11, 2014, from: http://www.publicinterestlawyers.co.uk/news_details.php?id=332

Ravenstone, Piercy (1824): *Thoughts on the Funding System and its Effects.* J. Andrews, London

Reed, H. (2012, February): "Credit Card Maxed Out?" How UK Debt Statistics Have Been Misrepresented. *Radical Statistics 107*, 4-14.

Reed, H. & Clark, T. (2013, April 4): *"Britain is Broke – We Can't Afford to Invest."* New Economic Foundation.

Reinhart, C. & Rogoff, K. (2010): *Growth in a Time of Debt. American Economic Review: Papers and Proceedings*, 100, 573-578.

Robinson, J. (1972). *The Second Crisis of Economic Theory*. The American Economic Review Vol. 62, No. 1/2 (Mar. 1, 1972), Published by: American Economic Association

Robinson, J. (1977). *What Are the Questions? Journal of Economic Literature*, 15(4), 1318-39.

Ro, S. (2013, August 8): *Every Country In Europe Should Be Glad It's Not Greece.* Retrieved April 21, 2014, from Business Insider:
www.businessinsider.com/european-gdp-since-pre-crisis-chart-2013-8

Rogers, S. (2012, June 30): *Healthcare spending around the world, country by country.* Retrieved April 28, 2014, from The Guardian:
www.theguardian.com/news/datablog/2012/jun/30/healthcare-spending-world-country

Rogers, S. & Sedghi, A. (2013, October 25): *UK GDP Since 1955.* Retrieved April 18, 2014, from The Guardian:
www.theguardian.com/news/datablog/2009/nov/25/gdp-uk-1948-growth-economy

Schaeffer, R. K. (Ed.) (2003): *Understanding Globalization: The Social Consequences of Political, Economic, and Environmental Change.* Rowman & Littlefield

Scrope, George Poulett (1831:; *The Political Economists.* Review of Malthus, Read and McCulloch for *The Quarterly Review* (Jan. 1831).

Skocpol, Theda (Ed.) (1984): *Vision and Method in Historical Sociology.* Cambridge: Cambridge University Press.

Skidelsky, R. (2014, March 17): *The Osborne audit: what have we learned?* Retrieved April 18, 2014, from New Statesman: www.newstatesman.com/politics/2014/03/osborne-audit-what-have-we-learned

Slavin, S.L. (2009): *Macroeconomics: Ninth Edition.* New York: McGraw-Hill.

Senior, Nassau (1836): *An Outline of the Science of Political Economy.* George Allen and Unwin reprint *(London, 1951) of* 1836 1st edition.

Stewart, M. (1986): *Keynes and After.* Penguin.

Stewart, H. (2013, November 13): Is Britain's economy really on the path to prosperity? Retrieved April 18, 2014, from The Observer: www.theguardian.com/uk-news/2013/nov/30/economy-osborne-autumn-statement-prosperity

Taleb, N.N. (2009): *Bloomberg News Interview.* Retrieved April 28, 2014, from YouTube: https://www.youtube.com/watch?v=krU1wPb7i6c

Thomson, A. (2012, November 5): *G20 eases push for deficit cutting.* Retrieved April 20, 2014, from Financial Times: www.ft.com/cms/s/0/c68ff436-279b-11e2-abcb-00144feabdc0.html#axzz2zRMaoN1r

Tsakalatos, E. (2005): *Homo Economicus and the Reconstruction of Political Economy: Six Theses on the Role of Values in Economics. Cambridge Journal of Economics*, Vol 29, Issue 6, 893-908.

UK Parliament. (2015): *Eurosceptic effect at the European Parliament: Key issues for the 2015 Parliament.* [Online] Available at: https://www.parliament.uk/business/publications/research/key-issues-parliament-2015/foreign-affairs/european-parliament/_[Accessed 3 4 2018].

Umuna, C. (2016): *Its official – there's a £200 million hole in the Brexit bus promise.* [Online] Available at: https://www.newstatesman.com/politics/staggers/2017/08/its-official-theres-200m-hole-brexit-bus-nhs-promise_[Accessed 5 4 2018]

Vina, G., Hutton, R & Penny. T. (2013, March 21): *Osborne Pledges Five More Years of U.K. Austerity.* Retrieved March 11, 2014, from: www.bloomberg.com/news/2013-03-20/osborne-pledges-five-more-years-of-u-k-austerity.html

Vlandas, Tim and Halikiopoulou, Daphne, (October 19, 2016): *Why Far Right Parties Do Well at Times of Crisis: The Role of Labour Market Institutions* ETUI Research Paper - Working paper 2016.07. Available at SSRN:
https://ssrn.com/abstract=2854926 or
http://dx.doi.org/10.2139/ssrn.2854926

Wadsworth, J., Dinghra, S., Ottaviano, G. & Reenen, J. (2016): *Brexit and the Impact of Immigration on the UK.* [Online] Available at: http://cep.lse.ac.uk/pubs/download/brexit05.pdf [Accessed 16 2 2018].

Warner, N. & O'Sullivan, J. (2014, March 31): *£10 each can save the NHS.* Retrieved April 28, 2014, from The Guardian: www.theguardian.com/commentisfree/2014/mar/31/10-pounds-each-save-nhs

Watt, N. (2012, September 30): *Tackle wasteful spending to earn second chance, Labour told.* Retrieved April 17, 2014, from The Guardian:
www.theguardian.com/politics/2012/sep/30/labour-second-chance-tackle-waste

Watt, N. & Mason, R. (2014, January 6): *Tories making 'monumental mistake' with lopsided cuts, says Nick Clegg.* Retrieved January 13, 2014, from The Guardian: www.theguardian.com/politics/2014/jan/06/tories-monumental-mistake-lopsided-cuts-nick-clegg

Wintour, P. (2013, September 9): *George Osborne claims economic argument is won: 'Britain is turning a corner'*. Retrieved April 24, 2014, from The Guardian: www.theguardian.com/politics/2013/sep/09/george-osborne-economy

Wintour, P., Monaghan. A & Osborne, H. (2014, January 30): *Living standards will not recover until after 2015 election says IFS.* Retrieved April 18, 2014, from The Guardian: www.theguardian.com/business/2014/jan/30/living-standards-not-recover-2015-ifs-miliband

Williamson, J. (2002): *What Washington Means by Policy Reform.* Retrieved April 16, 2014, from Peterson Institute for International Economics: www.iie.com/publications/papers/print.cfm?ResearchId=486&doc=pub

Wren-Lewis, S. (2013, September 25): *Sound Bite Economics.* Retrieved April 25, 2014, from: http://mainlymacro.blogspot.co.uk/2013/09/sound-bite-economics.html

Zagha, R. & Nankani, G. T. (Eds.). (2005): *Economic Growth in the 1990s: Learning from a Decade of Reform.* World Bank Publications.

Zimmerman, D. (2017): *Brexit, Trump and the media.* 1st edition. Abramis Publishing; United Kingdom.

Index of Names

	page
Adaman, F.	15, 17, 18.
Alesina, Alberto	27, 28, 30, 38-39, 56, 62, 82.
Amariglio, Jack	18.
Ardagna, Silvia	30-31, 56, 82.
Armitstead, L.	46.
Attlee, Clement	61-62.
Bagaria, Nitika	47-48.
Bălan, Sergiu	14, 20.
Balls, E.	13, 52, 80.
Barker, A.	72.
Becker, Gary	15.
Bell, D.	53-54.
Besley, T.	69.
Blair, T.	68.
Blanchard, Olivier	30, 46-49, 56.
Blanchflower, David	53-54.
Blyth, Mark	10, 42-44, 65, 69, 80-81.
Bowers, S.	72.
Boyer, Robert	33-35.
Brown, Gordon	21-22, 24, 68.
Buchanan, James	32, 43.
Cable, Vince	74.

Callari, A.	18.
Cameron, David	18-19, 48, 53, 75.
Carney, Mark	50, 55.
Chakraborrty, A.	77.
Chote, Robert	48, 55
Chowdhury, A.	44.
Clark, Thomas	61-62.
Clegg, Nick	74.
Conway, E.	49.
Darling, Alistair	22.
Day, Fred	14.
Dias, Dexter	77.
Drayton, Richard	64.
Duncan Smith, Iain	86.
Eaton, George	75.
Elliott, L.	27, 49, 51, 74.
Ford, R.	85-86.
Freud, *Lord, David*	33.
Friedman, Milton	16-17, 19, 31, 43.
Giavazzi, Francesco	27-30, 56.
Goodwin, M.	85-86, 88-89, 92, 96.
Gove, Michael	86.
Gray, John	16, 78-79.
Halikiopoulou, Daphne	87-88.
Heath, O.	85-86, 88-89, 92, 96.

Hellwig, Martin	29.
Hennessy, P.	69.
Hodgskin, Thomas	13, 14_N, 39-40, 42_N, 100-102.
Hopkin, J.	86, 89.
Hutton, Will	63-64.
Inglehart, R.	87-88.
Inman, P.	21, 61, 66.
Islam, I.	44.
Jakab, Zoltan	37-38.
Johnson, Simon	65.
Johnson, Boris	86.
Jorda, Oscar	46-47.
Kaletsky, Anatole	67.
Kates, Steven	38-39, 41.
Keynes, J.M.	7, 11-12, 16, 19, 28, 30, 33-37, 44, 67, 70, 73, 79.
Kendall, Liz	19.
King, Lawrence	31, 78-80.
King, Mervyn	66.
Koo, Richard	68.
Kumhof, Michael	37-38.
Kwak, James	65.
Laffer, Arthur	43.
Lagarde, Christine	48.
Laws, David.	71.
Lawson, Tony	20.

Leese, Richard	70.
Leigh, Daniel	46-48, 56.
Linton, D.	70.
Lucas, Robert	43.
Madra, Yahya	15, 17-18.
Major, John	68.
Mann, John	59.
Marx, Karl	19.
Mason, Rowena	74, 80.
McCulloch, J.R.	101.
McNulty, Roy	77.
Menger, Karl	42.
Mill, J.S.	41.
Miller, Maria	78.
Milne, Seumas	18, 53.
Monaghan, A.	51.
Monti, Mario	80.
Moya, E.	26.
Neumann, Manfred	29.
Norris, P.	87-88.
Osbourne, George	8_N, 11.
Pagano, Marco	27-30, 56.
Papademos, Lucas	80.
Pfeffer. C.	89.
Polanyi, Karl	14, 17-18, 20, 32_N, 89-90.

Portes, Jonathan	52, 55, 57-58.
Ravenstone, Piercy	39.
Reed, Howard	61-62, 68.
Reeves, Rachel	60.
Robinson, Joan	18, 36.
Rogers, S.	49, 76
Salisbury, *Lord*	64.
Say, Jean-Baptiste	32, 35, 38-39, 42.
Schularick, Moritz	47.
Scrope, G.P.	40.
Sedghi, A.	49.
Segal, Paul	60-61.
Senior, Nassau	40.
Skocpol, Theda	14_N.
Slavin, S.L.	36
Smith, Adam	14_N, 39.
Stewart, M.	50.
Taleb, Nassim Nicholas	71.
Taylor, Alan	46-47.
Thatcher, M.	32, 68, 90.
Thomson, A.	75.
Tobin, James	65.
Tsakalotos, Euclid	16.
Tullock, Gordon	43.
Turner, *Lord*	21.
Tyrie, Andrew	61.

Umunna, Chuka	86.
Vlandas, Tim	87-88.
Wadsworth, J.	87.
Warner, *Lord*	75-76.
Watt, Nicholas	19, 74.
Wintour, P.	54.
Wren-Lewis, Simon	58.
Zimmerman, D.	88.

www.ingramcontent.com/pod-product-compliance
Lightning Source LLC
Chambersburg PA
CBHW030625220526
45463CB00004B/1417